Tune

TUNE

by

IMOGEN HOLST

FABER & FABER

24 Russell Square

London

First published in mcmlxii
by Faber and Faber Limited
24 Russell Square, London, W.C.1
Printed in Great Britain by
Western Printing Services Ltd., Bristol

TO

THE MEMORY OF

SIR GEOFFREY FABER

1889–1961

In 1958 Sir Geoffrey Faber made a suggestion for a book called *Tune*, and it has been an exciting privilege to try to write what he wanted. He accepted the dedication, and the typescript was finished three months before his death, but he was too ill to read it, and I had no chance of telling him how grateful I was for his suggested title. As the book was written for his own pleasure it has escaped the uncomfortable necessity of having to 'cover a field'. The field, anyway, is too vast to be covered: it stretches too far into the distance, in time as well as in place. So there are immense gaps in the following chapters, and if Sir Geoffrey had been able to read them I am afraid he would have looked for many of his favourite tunes and failed to find them. But one or two of them are there, and I hope he would have enjoyed some of the others.

Aldeburgh   I.H.
April 1961

Contents

CHAPTER I

The Ingredients of a Tune

———— ◦∾⋙◦ ————

English musicians are fortunate to possess the word 'tune'. In America, where writers on music have been brought up in the German tradition, they are obliged to make do with 'melody' on every occasion, whether they are describing 'Sweet Polly Oliver' or the Adagietto from Mahler's fifth symphony. Americans are inclined to be scornful of our word 'tune', dismissing it as 'a popular term for any clear-cut and easily retained melody'. But their nineteenth-century German teachers would probably have been grateful if they could have borrowed the word in their attempts to explain the difference between 'melody' and 'melodies'. 'A child', wrote Schumann, 'sings his melodies [i.e. tunes] to himself; melody, however, is developed later in life.'[1]

Tunes are not only clear-cut and compact and easily remembered: they are also self-sufficient, and can sound completely satisfying when taken out of a context. A melody, in contrast to a tune, is inclined to spread itself intangibly. It is less easily held in the memory, and, from its very birth, it can be so deeply involved in what is going on all round it that it is seldom willing to live an independent life.

When Schumann said 'Melody is the amateur's war-cry', he must have been thinking of the innumerable music-lovers who had confessed to him that what they really liked was something with a *tune* in it. Schumann was one of the kindest of men, as well as one of the most enlightened of critics. He warned his own pupils in Leipzig to beware of despising the right kind of amateur,

[1] R. Schumann, *On Music and Musicians* (ed. K. Wolff), trans. P. Rosenfeld, Dennis Dobson, London, 1947, p. 236.

whose activities were inseparably bound up with the life of the professional artist. 'There has never been a time', he reminded them, 'when art has really flourished without this mutual give-and-take.' And he told his amateur listeners that he agreed with them that music without a tune was an impossibility: 'If, having stripped a work of its elaborations, we can still find a pure melody . . . [then] the composer has passed the test, and we will pay him our tribute.'[1]

It is encouraging to find, more than a hundred years later, that Stravinsky has been saying almost the same thing to his pupils in California:

> 'I am beginning to think, in full agreement with the general public, that melody must keep its place at the summit of the hierarchy of elements that make up music. Melody is the most essential of these elements . . . [It] survives every change of system.'[2]

To members of an audience, the great advantage of a tune is that it can be whistled in solitude. Many listeners find that a tune is all that remains when a performance is over. If the composer has offered his tunes whole and undisguised, they can be taken away as possessions and held securely in the memory. If he has woven them into an elaborate texture, it may not be possible to take away more than a fragment at the first hearing. But the fragment will prove to be memorable if the work has been worth listening to, for it will be the kernel of the music, and at each new hearing it will expand and grow clearer in the mind, until it reaches the miraculous stage of living a life of its own.

In spite of all attempts at analysis, the vitality of a tune is a miracle that can never be explained. It can only be marvelled at, as Roger North marvelled when he wrote:

> 'For the pleasing of a tune no reason hath bin given, that I know of; but yet I must think that there may be a fund discovered and layd open, out of which all pleasing tune in musick may be drawne. And altho' what is peculiarly good

[1] Schumann, op. cit., p. 76.
[2] Stravinsky, *Poetics of Music*, Vintage Books, New York, 1959, pp. 41 and 43.

hath come from thence, yet it hath bin fetcht out of the dark
. . . as it were by accident.'[1]

North has been criticized as a naïve and over-enthusiastic
amateur, but he knew enough about music to play trio sonatas
with Purcell, and in his notion of a fund 'discovered and layd
open' he was already pointing out the need for Mr. Deryck
Cooke's *The Language of Music*. The 'fetching out of the dark'
is a process that can be explored, for although the nature of a
tune can never be defined in words, it is possible to make a list
of a tune's ingredients. One of the most exhaustive of the recent
lists was made by Busoni in his 'Attempt at a Definition of
Melody':[2]

> 'A row of repeated ascending and descending intervals
> which, organized and moving rhythmically, contains in itself
> a latent harmony and gives back a certain atmosphere of
> feeling; which can and does exist independent of text for
> expression and independent of accompanying voices for form;
> and in the performance of which the choice of pitch and of
> instrument exercise no change over its essence.'

The word 'repeated', coming at the very beginning of this
definition of what we call 'tune', is a reminder of one of the
many advantages that notes have over words. Words can be repeated on rare occasions for some particular purpose, but music
thrives on repetition, and the same fragment can be repeated
over and over again without losing its meaning.

Busoni's sentence about the 'row of ascending and descending
intervals' is not as clear as it might be, because he forgets to
mention that the intervals can be step-wise or gapped, or a mixture of both. Cleonides, in the first century A.D., was able to be
more thorough than this, when he described gapped intervals as
a 'network'. It is an admirable word, suggesting the patterns of
sound in change-ringing, with each bell following its own course:

E D C
E C D

---

[1] *Roger North on Music* (ed. John Wilson), Novello, London, 1959, p. 110.
[2] F. Busoni, *The Essence of Music*, trans. Rosamond Ley, Rockliff, London,
1957, p. 33.

C E D
C D E
D C E
D E C

As raw material for making a tune, each pattern has its possibilities. When the changes are rung on F E D, the patterns gain a different meaning with the contrast between the tone and the semitone, and at G F E the new position of the semitone alters its relation to the tone and brings with it a new set of possibilities.

With four notes, change-ringing produces such a lavish supply of different patterns that it is almost bewildering to have to make a choice:

Ex. 1

The bar-lines in Ex. 1 are not real bar-lines: they are only marking the beginning of each row in the change-ringers' column of numbers. The music of the bells follows its own laws and creates its own satisfying beauty. But the printed patterns in Ex. 1 can never become tunes until they are organized and persuaded to move rhythmically. An up-beat can turn their first eight notes into the opening of a chorale:

Ex. 2

With six-eight instead of four-four, and 'Quick' instead of 'Slow', the same eight notes can be transformed into the beginning of a dance:

Ex. 3

When Busoni described 'a row of repeated ascending and descending intervals' as 'moving rhythmically', the word-order in his sentence demanded a comma to divide the two ingredients of pitch and time. But these two are inseparable. It is just as difficult to separate the rhythm from the intervals in a well-constructed tune as it is to separate the butter from the eggs in a well-cooked omelette.

The patterns in Ex. 1 are among the simplest that Busoni had in his mind when he said that intervals must be 'organized' before they could turn into tunes. Being a composer, he knew that finding the right interval was a matter of skilled reckoning. Yet there are many music-lovers who mistrust the word 'organized' when applied to tunes. They believe that 'the theme is a gift from heaven'. Their idea of a gifted composer is of one who writes in an emotional frenzy of inspiration: they forget that he is a practical man in very much the same position as that of a farmer or market gardener, who depends on his knowledge as well as on his instinct, and who knows by experience that gifts from heaven lead to a great deal of hard work and careful planning.

Planning involves ruthless pruning and selection. Everything has to be balanced and calculated. For instance, if the opening line of a chorale has to be built from the raw material of the patterns in Ex. 1, the choice of the first and second groups (Ex. 2) is not necessarily the best. The thirteenth pattern, followed by the third, might prove better:

Ex. 4

'Better' does not mean more pleasing in itself, but more suitable for the purpose. The chorale will need at least another six bars before it is complete, and these bars will want to extend beyond the range of the notes in Ex. 4, so the gradual rise from the lowest note may help to give a convincing shape to the eight-bar tune. And the drop of a fourth at the end of the first line of the hymn, coming after so many step-wise intervals, will emphasize the comma and help to make the form easy to grasp.

The purpose for which a tune is intended is one of the things a composer can never afford to lose sight of: it can prove to be his surest guide in the difficult task of calculated balancing. If he is a good enough composer, he will allow his knowledge and his instinct to work together in double harness, and the result of the process may well be what we call an 'inspired' tune.

Having insisted that the rhythmically moving intervals in a tune must be organized, Busoni goes on to say that a tune 'contains in itself a latent harmony'.

The trouble about the word 'harmony' is that it can mean so many different things. In its archaic Greek sense, the word *harmonia* 'stood for the enharmonic genus', Sachs tells us.[1] And 'the original *enharmonion* was pentatonic; its tetrachords had a major third with one uncleft semitone below'. This is the *pelog* mode of Java and Bali:

Ex. 5

By the time of Plutarch, *harmonia* could mean an elaborately

[1] C. Sachs, *The Rise of Music in the Ancient World*, Norton, New York, 1943, pp. 207 and 218.

constructed melodic line that had grown out of the few slow notes of a given theme.[1] 'Harmony' was still the agreeable joining together of melodic intervals that followed one after another. To the ninth-century writers of the *Scholia Enchiriadis*, who used the Greek word *symphonia* for the sounding together of vertical octaves, fifths and fourths, 'harmony' meant the agreeable blending of their parallel intervals. At the end of the sixteenth century, Thomas Morley was talking about 'the whole harmony of many voices' in his lessons on how to write tunes that could be sung in canon. Harmony had become polyphony. A hundred years later, the readers of Playford's *Introduction to the Skill of Musick* were given detailed instructions for composing in four parts: 'Let your Cords joyn as near to the Upper Part as they can, for the Harmony is [then] more agreeable to the ear.' Harmony meant chords, and the tune, for textbook purposes, had become an 'upper part'.

Chords were in Deryck Cooke's mind all the time he was writing *The Language of Music*, for he clearly states that he confined his investigation to the 'harmonic' period of musical history and to the tonal system 'derived from the vertical structure of music peculiar to Western Europe'. He dates his harmonic period from 'somewhere in the twelfth or thirteenth century'.[2] Busoni's date is very much later than that. When he says that a melody 'contains in itself a latent harmony' he is thinking of melodies since Bach; for in his essay *Von der Einheit der Musik*[3] he makes a passing reference to Gregorian chant and its 'complete absence of harmony', and then speaks of the oneness of the sort of music which 'exists as a living art', saying that it is 'already' to be found in the works of Bach. If, in 1961, it is difficult to agree that *every* tune contains a latent harmony, it is because there are more and more listeners who are discovering that Hindu ragas as well as Gregorian chants can still triumphantly exist as living works of art.

[1] '[In] Plutarch's . . . description of Olympos' composition *Nomos Athenâs* . . . the first movement is called *anpáeira* (practice, test) . . . and the main movement, *harmonia* . . . To one familiar with Oriental music, the passage suggests the principle of form preserved in Indian music to this day.' Sachs, op. cit., pp. 251 and 252.

[2] Deryck Cooke, *The Language of Music*, Oxford University Press, London, 1959, pp. xii, 40, 49.

[3] Busoni, op. cit., p. 2.

But even when Busoni's definition is limited to the period since Bach, his remark about latent harmony can only be accepted with reservations. It is true that rounds and canons carry with them their own harmony, which they spin like a web from their own tunes. And twelve-note themes evolve their self-contained harmony from the serial method of composition. But songs and dances and carols are not necessarily joined to *a* harmonization for life. The tune of 'Sweet Polly Oliver' spells out adequate harmonies while moving from one melodic interval to the next; but this does not mean that it is compelled to keep within the chords of its own vertical structure. A setting in free canon, with the second voice coming in a bar later and a fourth higher, is only one of the many unexpected but satisfying ways in which it could be harmonized. Busoni's definition needs, as a footnote, the remark made by Satie that 'a melody does not have *its harmony* any more than a landscape has *its colour*'.[1]

There can be no disagreement with the statement that a tune exists 'independent of text for expression and independent of accompanying voices for form'. The facts are irrefutable; the statement, however, sounds pale in comparison with the string of memorable tunes it brings into the mind. 'Oh, it is not to be described!' wrote Schumann in an ecstatic letter to Clara, when he had just heard the first try-through of Schubert's C major symphony, '*All the instruments are like human voices!*'[2] And the opening of that same symphony is a superb example of a tune that can exist naked and unsupported, having all the balance that is needed for conveying the vitality of its form.

'The choice of pitch and instrument exercises no change over the essence' of a tune. This is certainly true of pitch. The ancient Chinese were perhaps the only people who ever found it a matter of life and death to play at the correct pitch. They had to start their tunes at the 'absolute' pitch of their sacred bell: if the instruments were sharp or flat the whole dynasty was in danger of collapsing. In Europe, 'absolute' pitch is flexible enough to change from one generation to the next, according to the frequency that is in fashion at the time.

When Thomas Tomkins wrote down the exact measurement of

---

[1] Roger Shattuck, *The Banquet Years*, Faber & Faber, London, 1959, p. 131.
[2] *Schumann's Early Letters*, trans. May Herbert, Bell, London, 1888, p. 295.

one of the organ pipes he was using for his early seventeenth-century church music, he made it clear to future editors that Tudor motets would need to be transposed up a tone or a minor third if they were to be sung at about the same pitch as the secular madrigals. It is slightly upsetting to have to read Byrd in F minor instead of D minor, for the D flats look out of place in sixteenth-century music. But this is not nearly as bad as having to read some of the 'school editions' of works by Purcell or Gluck, where the music has been transposed down a semitone, to bring it, for the sake of the singers, to the eighteenth-century level of pitch. I shall never forget the look of despair on the faces of the second violins in an amateur orchestra when I had to ask them to play one of Gluck's beautifully simple tunes in the complicated key of A flat minor.

Experiments in tuning down to an earlier level of pitch are not always welcomed by the listeners. At a recent performance of Mozart's G minor piano quartet with an eighteenth-century forte-piano tuned a semitone below a' 440, some of the members of the audience insisted that the music sounded wrong when played at the wrong pitch. But it was Mozart's own pitch.

Today we are living under the threat of yet another rise in frequencies. If a' 440 is raised much further, the tessitura of some of the music written before the nineteenth-century will inflict too great a strain on professional singers as well as on amateurs, while instrumental tunes that were meant to sound effortless and mellow will acquire a hard, steely edge.

Busoni, when he mentioned 'choice of pitch', was probably not much concerned about changes of frequency. He was referring to the many transpositions of a tune that can occur in the answering voices of a cantata or a string quartet. These are the transpositions that help to extend the influence of a tune far beyond the boundaries of its own length. Tossed from one voice to another, answered a fifth higher here and a fourth lower there, one short phrase can become involved in more excitements than anyone except the composer could possibly have guessed from a first hearing of the straightforward, innocent notes.

Changing about in the 'choice of instruments' can also add to the excitement. It is only in unskilled 'arrangements' that a tune loses more than it can afford to lose. A violin solo rendered on a cornet can stretch a tune's adaptability almost to breaking-point. But good tunes can put up with an astonishing amount of ill-treatment. Their individuality is so strong that they can still be recognized, even when they are as grotesquely disguised as in the performance of Handel's 'Largo' on the musical saw, which I once had to adjudicate in the early years of what is now the Arts Council. A tune may suffer in the same kind of way that a water-colour suffers when it is badly photographed; but as long as it is recognizable its essence is unchanged. And this is true of piano reductions of orchestral works, though there are few things more frustrating than having to rob a flute tune of its flutter-tongue, or having to add unwanted tremolando chords to convey the crescendo of a sustained tune for strings.

In his sentence about choice of pitch and choice of instrument Busoni forgets to mention that a tune is not essentially changed when its speed is altered. Augmentation or diminution, in adding to the excitement of a work, can make the character of a tune stand out even more clearly than when it was first heard at its normal speed. It is only when the speed is unwittingly hustled owing to anxiety or unwillingly dragged owing to lack of control that the life of a tune is in danger. A lack of phrasing, that allows a tune no chance to breathe, can knock it senseless for the time being. But it is encouraging to find that intelligent slow practice is not harmful: the sound has a peculiar fascination of its own, like the fascination of watching swimmers diving or horses galloping in a slow-motion film.

In Busoni's definition there is only one sentence that is inadequate: it is his remark about the way in which a tune 'gives back a certain atmosphere of feeling'. This is far too vague for a description of what happens when a good tune is sung or played as its composer intended it to sound. It brings an atmosphere, it is true, but it also brings something much more satisfying and tangible. At the first hearing of a new tune, the moment of impact can be as welcome as a greeting or as stirring as a challenge. For tunes, like people, are startlingly individual. And there can be no end to the possibilities of getting to know them better.

CHAPTER II

Traditional Tunes

In the years just before the 1914 war two Victorian ladies, Miss Lucy Broadwood and Miss Juliet Williams, began collecting London street cries from the hawkers in Westminster and Chelsea. There was a broom-seller whom Miss Broadwood followed about for weeks on end, because his tune was so like the one Orlando Gibbons had quoted in his fantasia, *The Cries of London*.

> 'He is an elderly man', she wrote, 'with something gypsy-like and furtive about him. His voice is very true, ringing and musical, and his rhythm excellent, so that it is easy enough to take down the notes of his cry . . . [But] I could not catch one word that he sang . . .'[1]

The broom-seller had discovered, like other English singers, that in producing a long-drawn-out fortissimo there is little opportunity for pronouncing consonants. An Italian would have found no difficulty: a prolonged 'Sco—pe!' would have carried the length of the street without losing its meaning. But 'Brushes and brooms' are words that need the rhythm of their own sweeping gesture if they are to keep the vitality of their onomatopoeia.

The street-criers' tradition of leaving out consonants is an old one: Addison was complaining in *The Spectator* of December 1711 that the itinerant tradesmen of London cried 'so as not to be understood . . . People know the wares they deal in rather by their tunes than by their words.'

Miss Juliet Williams had the same difficulty in noting the cries.

---

[1] *Journal of the English Folk Song Society*, No. 22, p. 58.

She could tell that the man in Theobald's Road was trying to sell coal because she could see the coal in his cart, but his singing of the word 'coal'—even from a few yards away—sounded just like 'Ah mer! Ah mer!' She was more fortunate with the coal-man in Chelsea, who sang:

Ex. 6[1]

I can remember hearing this tune in Barnes in about 1912. The singer took it very slowly, dragging his feet along the road and stopping every few yards. His voice was fierce and lugubrious, and there was a ritual solemnity in his gestures that added to the memorableness of his tune.

Miss Williams's coal-man would have been astonished if she had told him that the musicologists considered his song 'logo-genic', that by singing on two notes he was 'using the melody as a mere vehicle for words', and that his tune, moreover, was an excellent example of cadential contrast, for, in the first word, his voice came to rest on the level that 'kept the listener in suspense', while at the second word it 'shifted to the other level to give a satisfactory ending'.[2] He himself was only concerned with getting through the day's work; he had found, like the rag-and-bone man in Ex. 7, that it was easier to keep going with a to-and-fro from one level to another:

Ex. 7

The slackening of the voice at the lower level conveys the leisurely question mark and allows the singer to recover enough energy to

[1] Examples 6–13 are taken from the *Journal of the English Folk Song Society*, Nos. 15 and 22.
[2] Sachs, op. cit., p. 41.

begin all over again. In Ex. 8, the queries alternate between a rising tension and a falling relaxation:

Ex. 8

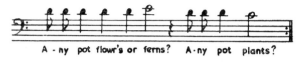

A conventional harmonization in C major could wreck the nicely adjusted balance of Ex. 8. The three notes are not in need of any seven-note scale to establish a relationship between them. They are entirely self-supporting, with D as their firmly established reciting note.

In 'Knives to grind?' (Ex. 9) the reciting note has to carry the query; it is helped by the spurt of energy it gains from the leap of the third:

Ex. 9

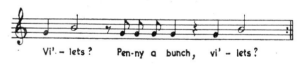

In Ex. 10 the leap upwards, away from the reciting note, makes the question sound more pressing and, at the same time, more hopeful:

Ex. 10

The leap of a fourth in Ex. 11 is still more insistent (the singer was selling clothes-props, but the cluster of consonants got in his way):

Ex. 11

23

The rising fifth in Ex. 12 must have had a lyrical quality when sung by 'an elderly man with a very sweet, full and melancholy tenor voice', who 'progressed slowly down Tachbrook Street in a small donkey-cart':[1]

Ex. 12

This phrase, with its sustained rhythm and its controlled dynamics, could be lifted out of its utilitarian surroundings and borrowed as a motive in an extended movement. Ex. 13, however, would be happier if left undisturbed, for it says all that needs to be said:

Ex. 13

This was sung by a small boy at Walthamstow in the 1880's. In the comparative quiet of the Essex countryside he was able to chant his words gently and persuasively, giving each phrase its natural rise and fall.

Nearly all the street-criers have given up long ago. Solitary survivors occasionally stray into the quieter corners of London—the Chelsea knives-and-scissors song can still be heard in Battersea—but most of the tunes have been forgotten. The odd assortment of goods they advertised, from lettuces and shrimps to chickweed for the bird, can all be ordered from the stores. And the roar of the traffic makes it impossible for any sweet-voiced elderly tenor to be heard.

[1] *Journal of the English Folk Song Society*, No. 22, p. 64.

In mountainous countries one can still hear the traditional wordless songs that reach from one side of a valley to the other, starting on a sudden high burst of energy and gradually relaxing downwards, as in the 'Juchzer' from the Steiermark in Ex. 14:

Ex. 14[1]

There is nothing useful about a 'Juchzer'. The singer is not trying to sell anything, nor is he calling the cattle home. The only practical purpose of his song is to celebrate the sheer enjoyment of having enough open space in which to express his exuberant feelings.

The Lappland herdsman who sang Ex. 15 must also have enjoyed the physical satisfaction of projecting his voice into a vast emptiness, although his wordless call was a necessary part of his daily work:

Ex. 15[2]

The most utilitarian of all open-air songs are the rhythmical action songs that have almost disappeared in Europe: they are no longer needed in an age of cranes and combine harvesters. But work-songs still exist in some other countries; Laurence Picken, in the *New Oxford History of Music*,[3] gives an example of a Chinese coolies' song that is nothing but a rhythmical give-and-take. 'It is an antiphon between leader and gang', he writes, 'in which statement and answer tread so closely on each other's heels that the sound is effectively continuous.' He suggests that Ex. 16 might be sung by men pulling a loaded cart up a hill:

---

[1] *Europäischer Volksgesang*, ed. W. Wiora, Arno Volk-Verlag, Köln.
[2] Ibid.
[3] *New Oxford History of Music*, Oxford University Press, London, vol. I, p. 131.

Ex. 16

Our nearest English equivalents to these action songs are the traditional singing games that are still occasionally acted in school playgrounds. The true *moto perpetuo* tunes are the dancing songs, such as Ex. 17:

Ex. 17[1]

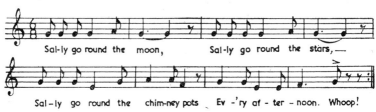

The singers in Ex. 17 skip round in a ring to the left, give a high kick at the 'whoop!', skip round to the right, another high kick, then back to the left, and so on, for at least ten minutes on end. When the rhythm has thoroughly got going it is extraordinarily difficult to break off and stop at a 'whoop': the fifteen skipping steps have generated so much energy that the dancers need to unwind in the opposite direction. As for the high kick, it is a perfectly timed moment of relaxation that combines the climax of excitement with the 'upbeat' preparation for a new beginning. Miraculously, the dancers have enough breath to keep on singing. The effortless to-and-fro gives a feeling of exhilaration, and while the tune lasts one can never grow weary of the perpetual movement.

The last of the English antiphonal work songs to survive were

[1] *Children's Singing Games*, ed. A. B. Gomme and Cecil Sharp, Novello.

the sailors' chanteys that flourished until steam spoilt them in the late nineteenth century. In the Woolwich version of 'Shallow Brown' (Ex. 18) the rhythmical continuity of statement and answer helps to shape the balanced phrases of the tune:

Ex. 18[1]

In narrative ballads it is the words that shape the tune. Each rise and fall has grown out of the words of the story in the Oxfordshire version of the ballad of Lord Bateman:

Ex. 19[2]

There are a hundred and eleven versions of this song in the *Traditional Tunes of the Child Ballads*,[3] and each tune has its own individuality. It was Kodály who said that in comparing folksong variants 'twenty or thirty tunes can be put side by side so that there will be hardly any difference between any two close-

---

[1] *Pulling Chanteys*, ed. Cecil Sharp, Novello.
[2] Cecil Sharp MS 4919.
[3] Ed. B. H. Bronson, Princeton University Press, 1959.

lying tunes, and hardly any similarity between the two furthest removed'. By the time the Oxfordshire 'Lord Bateman' has travelled to Aberdeenshire, the five-four has been tidied up into three-four, and the low-lying cadence at the end of the verse has been shifted to a more orthodox level:

Ex. 20[1]

Lord Bei-chan was a no-ble lord,— A no-ble-man of — high de-gree, And he has put his ship in or — der, A fo-reign coun-try to go and see.

And when the tune has reached a group of schoolchildren in Kentucky it is barely recognizable:

Ex. 21[2]

There was a man he liv'd in London, And he was of some high de-gree, He be-came un-ea-sy, dis-con-tent-ed, Some fair land, some land to see.

A folk song depends on its variations to keep it alive. Even when

[1] *Last Leaves of Traditional Ballads*, ed. Gavin Grieg and Alexander Keith. Buchan Club, Aberdeen, 1925.
[2] *Traditional Ballads Mainly from West Virginia*, ed. John H. Cox. National Service Bureau, New York, 1939.

it is sung by members of the same family there are individual turns of phrase that keep it as flexible as an improvisation. A version of the Somerset 'Seeds of Love' was sung to Cecil Sharp in 1904 by Jim Squires of Holford (Ex. 22). Nearly fifty years later his son William Squires was singing the version in Ex. 23:

Ex. 22[1]

I sow'd the seeds of love ____ And I sow'd them in the spring, ____ I ga-ther'd them up in the morn-ing so soon, While the small birds sweetly sing, ____ While the small birds do sweet-ly sing.

Ex. 23[2]

It is this flexibility that gives a folk song its anonymous character. As Maud Karpeles has pointed out,[3] a song is not anonymous 'merely because the original author has been forgotten, but because it has been fashioned and re-fashioned through many

---

[1] *Journal of the English Folk Dance and Song Society*, vol. VIII, No. 4.
[2] Ibid.
[3] *Grove's Dictionary of Music and Musicians*, Macmillan, London, 1954, vol. III, p. 183.

generations by countless individual singers, and of these singers the contribution of the first may be no greater than that of the last'.

But what about the contribution of the first singer? Where did he get the tune from? This is the question Vaughan Williams asked a Mr. Pottipher of Ingrave, Essex, when he was collecting folk songs from him in 1904. Mr. Pottipher replied: 'If you can once get the words, the Almighty sends you a tune.'

The anonymous Kentucky singer who first thought of 'Nottamun Town' (Ex. 24) would probably have agreed with Mr. Pottipher:

Ex. 24[1]

In Not-ta-mun Town not a soul would look up, Not a soul would look up, not a soul would look down, Not a soul would look up, not a soul would look down To tell me the way to Not-ta-mun Town.

How did the first singer of this song manage to balance his motives as satisfactorily as if he had been trained to organize them? It is easy to accept 'Co-erl' and 'Any pot-flow'rs or ferns?' as instinctive reciting tunes that happened by themselves. But there are intervals in 'Nottamun Town' that sound as if they have been drawn out of the 'fund of all pleasing tune' with a calm and secure deliberation. It is the same security that enables the American Indians to make a leap of a seventh in their 'Fireweed Song'[2] in Ex. 25 where the pentatonic intervals move rapidly up and down in a pattern that suggests the familiarity of long experience:

[1] *Seventeen Nursery Songs from the Appalachians*, ed. Cecil Sharp, Novello.
[2] Marius Barbeau, 'Asiatic Survivals in Indian Songs', *Musical Quarterly*, January 1931.

Ex. 25

Yaw haw hee haw law ho – lee, ha – e lee – ho – ee – yae,

A search for the origin of this assured familiarity would probably lead us back as far as Adam. Adam, according to Peter
Pears,[1] was the first tenor. Having a great deal of space to practise
in, and being as yet unburdened by any worries, it is probable
that his first song was in the nature of a 'Juchzer':

Ex. 26

This is the kind of song that Curt Sachs calls 'pathogenic'·
'Music', he writes, 'is often due to an irresistible stimulus that
releases the singer's utmost possibilities. . . . He lends all his
force and passion to the beginning of the song, and lets his melody
drop as his vocal chords slacken. . . . Descending melodies . . .
may have come from such unbridled outbursts.'[2] Sachs goes on to
mention that in aboriginal tunes from Central and South
Australia the descending phrase is often pentatonic without semitones, and the intervals of the fourth and fifth begin to stand out
as landing-stages. This is the shape of tune that is also sung by
the Papuans in New Guinea (Ex. 27):

Ex. 27[3]

etc.

---

[1] *Words and Music*, a broadcast talk.

[2] Sachs, op. cit., p. 41.

[3] Jaap Kunst, *A Study on Papuan Music*, quoted in *New Oxford History of
Music*, vol. I, p. 178.

And there is a beautiful example of antiphonal pentatonic singing from Annam, sung by a water-man and his wife:

Ex. 28[1]

The landing-stages of fourths and fifths in these descending tunes give security to singers who are fetching their songs out of the dark. After a while, the shape of the pentatonic mode becomes so familiar that it is easy for the American Indians to dip into it and extract what they need for their 'Fireweed Song' (Ex. 25). It is from a pentatonic mode that the Kentucky singer draws out the balanced phrases of 'Nottamun Town' (Ex. 24), and the Woolwich sailors find their statement and answer for 'Shallow Brown' (Ex. 18).

In his *Folk Music of Hungary*,[2] Kodály quotes pentatonic tunes that are sung by the Mari, who live in the Volga region of Hungary. Their pentatonic scale, descending E D B A G E, is the form which, he says, 'appears to be native to Turkish-Tartar peoples living in the Russian wastes as far as China'.

The Mari tunes begin high, with the first phrase repeated a fifth lower:

---

[1] G. Knosp, *Histoire de la Musique dans l'Indo-Chine*, quoted in *New Oxford History of Music*, vol. I, p. 158.
[2] Barrie & Rockliff, 1960.

Ex. 29[1]

This shape suggests the two levels of antiphonal singing; it is as if the pattern of statement and answer had become so deep-rooted that it was necessary to follow it, even with a solo voice. The pattern, however, is only another variant of a 'Juchzer' descent through the pentatonic mode.

Sometimes the first half of a Mari tune uses a note that cannot be answered a fifth lower because it would be outside the mode. When this happens, the singer instinctively alters the pattern, singing the nearest note within the mode, as in the second bar of the answer in Ex. 30:

Ex. 30

To the eye of those who have been brought up on harmony and on the analytical difference between a tonal and a real answer, this looks like a mental adjustment. But the Mari singer was not concerned with rules. He was keeping strictly to the mode because the sound of its pattern was so familiar that it had become part of him.

In Ex. 31 the singer chooses to adjust the level of the notes in bars 5 and 6, although an exact answer at the fifth would have been within the mode:

---

[1] Examples 29–36 are taken from Z. Kodály, *Folk Music of Hungary*, Barrie & Rockliff.

Ex. 31

Here again the analytically-minded reader is tempted to think that the adjustment implies an underlying harmony and a sense of 'key' in our meaning of the word. But the Mari singer was not thinking in chords. He was obviously aware of the strong mutual attraction of the tonic and the fifth above it: he felt it in his bones, because he was so used to the sound of the bagpipes.

The Mari songs sometimes vary the pattern of the first half of the tune, descending in a long curved line:

Ex. 32

In Ex. 33, which is a Hungarian version of a Mari tune, the high opening line of the long curve has been brought down an octave, forming the arched shape of many English folk songs:

Ex. 33

It is what Schneider[1] has called 'the progressive breaking away

---

[1] *New Oxford History of Music*, vol. I, p. 23.

from the given motive' that helps to create the continuity of a primitive tune. As soon as the basic pattern of the Mari song has been transformed into a curving arch, there can be any number of possible variants:

Ex. 34

The long notes at the end of each bar in Ex. 34 are like the landing-stages of tunes in the Far East, where the gong-player travels slowly up and down the mode, embroidering each note in turn by approaching it from above and from below, varying the rhythmic patterns of twos and threes and finding in the variations enough ingredients to last for a lifetime. In music such as this, the mode *is* the tune.

By keeping instinctively to the notes of the pentatonic mode and varying the approach to each note, the Mari singers are able to balance the phrases in Ex. 35, achieving, like the Woolwich sailors in 'Shallow Brown', what appears to be a miracle of calculated organization:

Ex. 35

Kodály mentions that the Hungarian version of Ex. 35 ends on E, but he thinks that many Hungarian tunes which today end on the E would at one time have ended on the D, which is the version that is more usual in the East. It is the D-ending which makes

Ex. 35 sound like a Scottish folk song. If the tune found its way into an album of Scottish songs with conventional accompaniments it would probably be harmonized in G major, with its last note as the 'upper part' of a tonic chord, and its last bar but one as a chord of C, to provide the tranquil satisfaction of a plagal cadence. This is the way many Scottish tunes are harmonized, and it is a way that can sound beautiful. But the chord of C has no business in Ex. 35, for C is outside the Mari mode.

It would be futile to cling to these pentatonic tunes and try to keep them pure. Folk songs depend for their continued existence not only on their variants but also on their arrangements. And if Luther had not borrowed modal German love songs and distorted them by turning them into four-part congregational hymns we might never have had Bach's *St. Matthew Passion*. But we need the best of both worlds, and now and then it is good to meet a primitive tune that has kept free from all associations. In Deryck Cooke's *The Language of Music*, which is concerned with vertical harmony, the rising sixth in Ex. 35 would be given an expressive meaning in relation to the triad that is spelled out by the notes in bars 1, 2 and 4. But triads are not the beginning and end of music. To the Mari singer, this rising sixth would have had an entirely different expressive meaning. For him, nothing was spelled out but the intervals of the pentatonic mode. And there was no need to spell them, for they were already lying waiting, at the core of all his tunes.

The link between the harmonically-minded European and the pentatonically-minded Mari is more easily to be found in Ex. 36, which is a Hungarian major version of the traditional Mari pattern:

Ex. 36

Kodály says that it is such tunes as this, with their counterparts in Czech, Slovak and Polish folk music, that 'link the Western tonal system to the Eastern-derived construction'.[1] He also says:

'The pentatonic system was able to develop among peoples who had no mutual contact, such as African Negroes, North American Indians, Celts, Chinese, etc. But striking and essential correspondence in melodic construction, phraseology and rhythm is far from accidental. Here contact or common origin must be assumed . . . Since the germ of pentatonic tunes, and the most frequently occurring groups of notes are the three neighbouring notes (in the examples G A B), it is quite easy to imagine the pentatonic scheme arising from a reciting formula of this three-note range. The great mass of primitive examples does not go beyond the range of three notes. They begin on the first, stay on the third or possibly the second for a long time, and end by descending to the first. More developed forms touch the fifth above the opening note at one or two strongly accented points; for a more emphatic conclusion they descend to the third below the opening note. . . .'[2]

Kodály quotes examples of Hungarian tunes which follow this pattern, and he compares them with a Gregorian chant:

Ex. 37

'This tune-type', says Kodály,[3] 'cannot be regarded as a primitive Finno-Ugrian or Turkish type . . . it is not the property of one or two peoples, but has, so to speak, achieved international currency throughout the East . . . [And] these peoples can scarcely have derived it from either the Christian or the Jewish [liturgy] . . . It seems to embody some more general, supranational, archaic reciting formula.'

[1] Kodály, op. cit., p. 37.
[2] Ibid., pp. 54 and 55.
[3] Ibid., p. 53.

CHAPTER III

Plainchant

————— ᘓᘏᘏᘏᘓ —————

Gregorian reciting-tones were made for use, not for ornament. As with street cries, their memorable patterns have grown from the practical need for making the human voice audible at a distance.

Spoken words get lost in the maze of echoing overtones that can haunt catacombs and cathedrals. But when the voice prolongs each word at a clearly held level of pitch, the imprisoned reverberations welcome the sound and their conflicting murmurs of protest are quietened as if by magic.

The laziest way of transforming speech into song is to chant each word on the same note. The earliest singers of plainsong, however, had no use for this monotonous kind of singing. They had probably learnt by trial and error that a single-note chant, though needing less disciplined concentration, is far more exhausting in the end, for it lacks the give-and-take of a two-note chant such as 'Co-erl!' or 'Any rag or bones?', where the relaxation at the cadence stores up new energy for continuing. And in a sung statement and answer, such as 'The Lord be with you': 'And with thy spirit', a single-note chant lacks the graciousness of the balanced to-and-fro in Ex. 38:

Ex. 38[1]

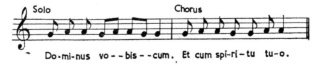

Do-mi-nus vo- -bis- -cum. Et cum spi-ri-tu tu-o.

[1] All Gregorian chants in this chapter are transcribed from the Vatican text.

This is one of the chants described as 'ancient tones' in the *Liber Usualis* of Gregorian chants. Many of them are founded on the traditional pentatonic pattern that Kodály mentions as having achieved international currency throughout the East. Centred on the three notes G, A and B, the chants occasionally dip down to the E for emphasis, as in the response 'Let us bend the knee' in Ex. 39:

Ex. 39

In these earliest chants, the members of the congregation would have had no difficulty in finding the E, owing to their long familiarity with the mode.

The ancient *Gloria XV* in Ex. 40 shapes its arched phrase from the same familiar formula:

Ex. 40

Here the tone has already become a tune. And in the cadential formula for a full stop in Ex. 41 the pentatonic pattern achieves a memorable beauty while fulfilling its strictly utilitarian purpose of warning the listeners when to come in with their 'Amen':

Ex. 41

In some of the early chants the 'Amen' was sung at the end of every line of a prayer, following the Jewish tradition that is clearly shown in Deuteronomy xxvii, verses 15 to 26; 'And all the people shall say, Amen.' This was the tradition of the mid-second-century *Hymn of Jesus* quoted in the apocryphal Acts of St. John:[1]

> 'He bade us therefore make as it were a ring, holding one another's hands, and himself standing in the midst he said: Answer Amen unto me. He began then to sing an hymn and to say:
> Glory be to thee, Father.
> And we, going about in a ring, answered him: Amen.
> Glory be to thee, Word: Glory be to thee, Grace. Amen.'

In the earliest known chant to the Lord's Prayer, a Mozarabic version which may date from the fourth century, the 'Amen' comes at the end of each line:

Ex. 42[2]

The repeated Amens have disappeared from the later Gregorian *Pater Noster* that is still sung (Ex. 43), but the tune has kept its ancient outline:

Ex. 43

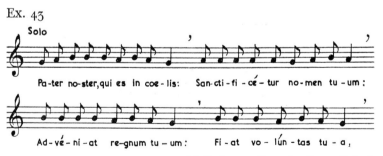

---

[1] *Apocryphal New Testament*, trans. M. R. James, Clarendon Press, Oxford, 1953, p. 253.
[2] *New Oxford History of Music*, vol. II, p. 82.

Sic - ut in coe - lo, et in ter - ra. Pa - nem no-strum quo-ti- di - á - num da no-bis hó - di - e: Et di - mít-te no-bis dé - bi - ta no-stra sic - ut et nos di-mít- ti-mus de-bi - tó - ri -bus no-stris. Et ne nos in - dú -cas in ten - ta - ti - o - nem, Sed lí-be- ra nos a ma - lo.

Chorus

The tune is a miracle of economy, with its three-note phrases balancing the rise and fall of the words, and its single descent to E serving as a cue to warn the listeners when to sing the response. The anonymous 'composer' was a genius in stringing together the well-worn formulas that had been used over and over again in both Jewish and Christian liturgy.

The Jewish three-note chants used the rising and falling patterns in strict alternation, varying the length of the phrases according to the number of words in each line:

Ex. 44[1]

Way-yo - sha a - do- nay _____ ba - yom ha hu _____

et Yis - ra - - el _____ *etc.*

'The ancient melodic unit was the step,' says Curt Sachs. 'The Jews understood melodic movement as composed of "motives" in the true sense of the word.'

[1] Sachs, op. cit., p. 83.

The motives were there, ready-made, for Christians as well as for Jews. Wellesz has described[1] how the musicians in the early Byzantine church were told to keep strictly to the familiar patterns in their chants, because these were phrases that had been 'transmitted by the angels to prophets and inspired saints'. Jewish musicians referred to each of their motives by name: a rising fourth could be called 'preceding'; a step-wise descent, 'broken'; a long repeated note, 'stretcher', and a slow mordent, a 'hand's breadth'.[2] In their cadences they kept rigidly to the rules of punctuation, slurring the falling second before a semicolon or a full stop in obedience to a law of Hebrew grammar that demanded a prolonged syllable in the last word of a sentence.[3] This is the cadential slur at 'temptation' and 'evil' in Ex. 43. But it would be difficult to say whether the slur was following the tradition of Hebrew grammar or following the instinctive expression of voice that can be heard in the cadences of songs written in every century from then until now. In plainchant, as in other great music, instinct and reason get so mixed up that it is impossible to separate them.

The seemingly instinctive form of the Gregorian antiphon may well have been borrowed from Hebrew recitation. The first line of an antiphon is repeated, word for word, at the end of the chant. (This is a custom that often puzzles non-Catholics: they find it strange that a line such as 'Thou shalt purge me with hyssop and I shall be clean' should be sung all over again after the 'Glory be to the Father' has already come to an end.) Musically, this return is one of the most satisfying of all forms. We are so used to it, from the Middle Ages to the present day, that it is almost impossible to imagine a time when tunes were not this shape. But the earliest antiphons repeated their opening sentence after each line, as if following one of the Jewish methods of congregational singing, by which the rabbi or leader would begin by singing the first half-line, with the congregation repeating it: the leader would go on half a line at a time, while the congregation kept to the same words, as in Psalm 136: 'For his mercy endureth for ever.'

---

[1] E. Wellesz, *A History of Byzantine Music and Hymnography*, Clarendon Press, Oxford, 1949, p. 52.

[2] Sachs, op. cit., p. 84.

[3] See E. Werner, *The Sacred Bridge*, Dennis Dobson, London, 1959, p. 433.

Jewish music, according to Idelsohn, has lived for four thousand years. 'The tradition is preserved in practice in various Jewish centres including Yemen in South Arabia, . . . a community that lived practically in seclusion for thirteen hundred years . . . in Babylonia, . . . dating from the destruction of the first Temple, . . . and in Persia, [where the tradition] is almost as old as in the Babylonian community.'[1]

In these Jewish congregations Idelsohn found exact counterparts of Gregorian chants. Several of these chants are in the ancient tones of Exs. 38–43, the 'supranational' mode that Clement of Alexandria called the *tropos spondeiakos* when he recommended it to Christian singers in the second century. (It is just possible that this is the mode in which Christ chanted in the synagogue when he read verses from Isaiah, as described in Luke iv, v. 16–20. The words had to be sung, not spoken, for the Jewish law insisted that the Bible 'should be read in public and made understood to the hearers in a musical, sweet tune'.[2])

There are Jewish and Gregorian parallels in other modes, including an almost identical version of the *Tonus Peregrinus* (Exs. 45–6) for Psalm 113 (114), 'When Israel came out of Egypt, the house of Jacob from among the strange people.'

Ex. 45[3]

B -tzeth Yis-ra-el mi-mitz-ra-yim, beth Ya'a-kov me-'am lo-ez ___

Ex. 46

In ex-i-tu Is-ra-el de Ae-gyp-to, do-mus Ia-cob de po-pu-lo bar-ba-ro.

The mode is no longer pentatonic, for the semitone has found its way in. As with many of the Hungarian variants of Kodály's

[1] A. Z. Idelsohn, *Jewish Music*, Tudor Publishing Co., New York, 1948, p. 22.
[2] Ibid., p. 35.
[3] Werner, op. cit., p. 419.

Mari folk songs, the semitone began transforming the *tropos spondeiakos* by entering unobtrusively as a falling passing-note:

Ex. 47[1]

Tu man-da-sti (etc.)   man-da-ta tu - a :   cu - sto - di - ri   ni — mis.

The potency of a falling semitone has become so bound up with harmony that we need to get rid of the sound of a suspension when listening to the expressive cadence in Ex. 48:

Ex. 48

Al - le - lu - ia.

Syllabic Alleluias are rare in plainsong, for the word cries out for the long line of a melisma. A Gregorian Alleluia is the Church's equivalent of a 'Juchzer', with the final syllable prolonged to a wordless *jubilus* of exuberation:

Ex. 49

Al - le - lu — — — ia

'Jubilare est rustica voce inclamare', wrote Paul the Deacon in the eighth century, acknowledging plainsong's debt to folk song.[2] Four hundred years before him, St. Hilary had said: 'We give the name "jubilus" to the call of a shepherd or farm worker, when in a lonely place his voice, calling or answering, is plainly

[1] W. Apel, *Gregorian Chant*, Burns & Oates, London, 1958, p. 212.
[2] See G. B. Chambers, *Folksong-Plainsong*, Merlin Press, London, 1956, p. 22.

heard because the sound is long-drawn-out and pitched to carry.'[1]

The long-drawn-out melismas of the *jubilus* helped to transform simple reciting tones into elaborate melodic lines, where each note of the modal phrase could be embroidered with minute detail and extravagant repetition:

Ex. 50

Apel, in his book on Gregorian chant,[2] quotes this 'Jubilate' as 'representing the utmost degree of boldness' that is to be found in the language of plainsong. Later, he refers to the 'reiterative' style of many of the chants, a style that turns the descending cadential formula of A G F E into the more elaborate line in Ex. 51:

Ex. 51

'It is this style', Apel says, 'which, rightly or wrongly, has often been called "oriental". Whether oriental or not, it is indeed far removed from the basic concepts of the western mind, as appears from the fact that our vocabulary has only more or less derogatory terms to indicate it: . . . prolixity, diffuseness etc., all indicative or suggestive of a lack of conciseness.' But it is only to those who think perpetually in terms of harmony, whether 'conventional' or serial, that the repetition of Ex. 51 seems redundant. To the Indian singer or player, this persistent twisting

---

[1] 'in nisum sonus'.
[2] Apel, op. cit., p. 257.

and twining round the main intervals of a cadence is one of the essential ways of unfolding the theme.

European listeners feel more at home when melismas move step-wise up and down, as in Ex. 52:

Ex. 52

Here the syllabic skeleton of F C D is clothed in a manner that seems 'natural' to us, because it is like the familiar kind of melisma that can be found in almost any aria by Handel:

Ex. 53[1]

If the plainsong melisma in Ex. 52 is phrased in an unbroken line, there can be no danger of the word losing its meaning, for the final syllables emerge at the end of the long line with their own spoken rhythm unimpaired.

In phrasing plainsong, the freely flowing rhythm is helped by the ligatures that prolong the stressed syllables, as in Ex. 54:

Ex. 54

The shape of this sentence sounds as if it has grown inevitably from the sense of the words, with its rising tension for the calling out, and its relaxation when the cry has been heard.

There are hundreds of examples of this expressive shaping of a phrase, where the words seem to convey a gesture, as in the anxiety of Ex. 55 and the satisfaction of Ex. 56:

---

[1] From *L'Allegro*: 'And ever against eating cares.'

Ex. 55

Li - - be - ra me Do - mi - ne

Ex. 56

De - o gra - ti - as

The idea of Gregorian 'word-painting' is sternly condemned by Apel in his book.[1] He disapproves of the suggestion that the setting of the words 'et turtur' in Ex. 57 is meant to imitate the cooing of the turtle-dove:

Ex. 57

et tur - - tur ni - - dum

This setting of *turtur*, Apel says, is 'the result, not primarily of the imagery of the words, but of their spelling, there being always two consonants after each vowel'. He does not mention, however, that onomatopoeia has been the cause of the spelling as well as of the phrasing. A spoken 'turtur' is already a cooing sound.

In plainsong, as in folk song, the words and the tune are so inseparable that it is useless to try to pull them apart. In both plainsong and folk song, the rise and fall of the first verse proves, over and over again, to belong just as much to the twentieth verse. And for this rise and fall, the anonymous 'composers' managed to find a limitless wealth of variety within the bounds of their chosen mode.

The Gregorian modes were never influenced by any of the oriental scales. Idelsohn[2] has pointed out that the Jews did not

[1] Op. cit., p. 303.
[2] Op. cit., p. 87.

use a mode with an augmented second until after the Mongols and Tartars had joined them at the beginning of the thirteenth century; and this was far too late to have had any effect on the development of Gregorian chant. In the European countries that were occupied by Turks or Arabs, the interval of the augmented second crept into some of the native folk songs, afterwards becoming entangled with the tunes that were brought by the gypsies. But church music remained aloof, finding all the intervals it needed in the 'white-note' modal scales.

'Exotic' is the name that we give to the scales with augmented seconds in them. And because 'exotic' has come to mean 'outlandish and barbarous', the interval of the augmented second is sometimes considered 'unnatural'.

'We Westerners are in the habit of thinking that the European tonal system is the only true one,' said Jaap Kunst in a recent talk on *gamelan* music.[1] '[We think] that all other systems which deviate from ours are incorrect and untrue, not to say primitive or even perverse. This opinion is based entirely upon convention, tradition and mental indolence.'

There are certainly many possible ways of shaping two tetrachords in an octave, and no one who has sat at the feet of musicians in India can feel that there is anything unnatural in the sound of the augmented second.

[1] Kongress-Bericht, Internationale Gesellschaft für Musikwissenschaft Utrecht, 1952, p. 272.

CHAPTER IV

Ragas[1]

There was nothing exotic about the first tune I heard sung in India. It might almost have been a Gregorian chant:

Ex. 58

The tune floated up from the courtyard at the back of the house, sung gently but with firmness and persistence. The number of syllables changed with each verse, but the tune itself remained the same, and it went on for at least half an hour. I was told the next morning that the boy who helped in the kitchen had been chanting verses from the Rig Veda.

This was at Santiniketan, the university founded by Tagore in West Bengal. During Gandhi's last visit there he had reminded the students that their university was meant to be international, and had told them that they should try to learn something about western music. After his death, the teaching staff felt it was their duty to do what he had suggested. They asked Leonard Elmhirst for his advice, and as I happened to be working for him at that time, I had the good fortune to be sent to Santiniketan as a pupil-teacher.

It was December, and my pupils, who had been brought up to sing their tunes at the right season of the year, asked if they

---

[1] Throughout this chapter Indian musical terms are written without accents.

might learn some Christmas music. So we began with the plain-song Allelulia that Britten uses in his *Ceremony of Carols*, counting the notes in the familiar Hindu rhythm of eleven time-units:

Ex. 59

Al - le - lu - - - - - ia,　　Al - le - lu - - - - - ia.

It sounded magnificent when sung over and over again, with immense emphasis, to the Indian equivalent of tonic-solfa: 'SA-SA-*SA*-SA-DHA-PA-SA-RI-SAAA, SA-RI-*SA*-GA-RI-GA-SA-RI-SA-SAA.'

The Sa Ri Ga names were a help in exchanging folk songs. We kept to pentatonic tunes at first, because they always sounded familiar, whichever side of the world they had come from. Sometimes the tunes we had chosen to give each other were like variants of the same song: on the morning when my teacher sang me the Punjabi tune in Ex. 60, I had brought him the Kentucky tune in Ex. 61:

Ex. 60

Quick

Tu Tha – gi　a ccha ri　ye,　Tu Tha – gi　ve,　Bo le

Kho Ta de ra　Pai　ye mu ye　Tu Tha – gi　ve.

Ex. 61[1]

Quick

I　gave my love a cher-ry　that　has　no　stones, I

[1] *English Folk Songs from the Southern Appalachians*, vol. **II**. Collected Cecil Sharp, edited Maud Karpeles. Oxford University Press, London, 1932.

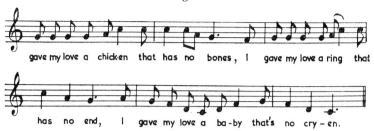

gave my love a chicken that has no bones, I gave my love a ring that has no end, I gave my love a ba-by that's no cry-en.

The folk tunes were not always so easy to learn. Coming home in the dark evenings, the students used to sing Bengali folk songs which would suddenly break off on a staccato leading-note: it took nearly a fortnight before I got used to it and stopped wondering what had gone wrong.

The rhythms were more bewildering than anything else, and I never got much further than the beginners' class, where we clapped one-in-a-bar to the Children's Song in Ex. 62, having learnt the tune the Indian way, by ear:

Ex. 62

The claps were silent, and, as in African music, they only existed in the background, without adding any rhythmical effect to the tune itself.

The drum-rhythms in the classical music were far too difficult to follow. My teachers would sit round me while we were listening to a raga, and would mutter encouragingly: 'Tala Tivra; seven matras. Count seven!' But as soon as they stopped counting with me I lost the beginning of the sevens.

Equally bewildering, at first, was the unexpected style of the singing. I knew in theory that 'for the Far Eastern musician singing is opposed to speech: the voice is used like a highly-strung instrument'.[1] But theoretical knowledge was no protection against the shock of hearing such extraordinary sounds. The first soloist I listened to seemed to be singing variations on the *jubilus* in Ex. 50 (page 45) but in a fierce and rapid fortissimo, with sudden passionate crescendos and harsh, rasping pauses on the high notes, and, worst of all, with gurgling glissandos that slid slowly down from one landing-stage to the next. It was five or six days before I could feel quite sure that the singing was neither primitive nor perverse. Hearing the same kind of sounds day after day, I found that the style began to grow familiar and inevitable. The harshness of the high notes became appropriate, and I was able to welcome the portamentos as soon as I had realized that each slide belonged to a particular level of pitch in the microtonal tuning of the intervals. Before leaving England I had read in Alain Daniélou's textbook[2] that 'a normal ear can easily perceive sixty-six distinct intervals within the compass of an octave', and that 'among the sixty-six intervals, twenty-two are chiefly used in music'. And, dealing in twenty-two rather than sixty-six microtones, I had memorized the tuning of the Bileval scale, which is the Indian equivalent of our major scale:

1	2	3	4	5	6	7	8	9	10	11	12	13	14	15	16	17	18	19	20	21	22

SA	RI	GA	MA	PA	DHA	NI
C	D	E	F	G	A	B

But the pitch of each individual note in the scale can have no meaning until it is heard with the Sa, for 'without a relation to Sa, an isolated sound cannot be called a note'.[3] Throughout the long melodic improvisation of a classical raga, the Sa can be heard on the plucked strings of the tampura, like an ethereal drone. It is a reassuring sound, and it can never be lost.

Each interval that is heard in relation to Sa has its own expression in performance, an expression that changes according to the microtonal size of the different intervals in each modal scale.

When the octave is divided into sixty-six microtones there are

---

[1] *New Oxford History of Music*, vol. I, p. xix.

[2] Alain Daniélou, *Northern Indian Music*, vol. I, Christopher Johnson, London, p. 45.

[3] Ibid., p. 45.

three possible levels for A flat in relation to C, and four for F sharp. If the flattest A flat moves down to the sharpest F sharp before relaxing on to the G, the portamento linking the A flat and F sharp has its own particular timing and dynamic emphasis which belong by rights to that one interval.

Expression and intonation are the same thing in Indian music. The trained listener can follow each subtlety in the melodic line in the same way in which we can enjoy the harmonies in a Bach fugue; while even the untrained listener with an indifferent western ear can make a guess at the pitch of the intervals by recognizing the expression of the slides and shakes and turns.

I found it impossible to memorize fragments of a raga during a performance; the music was too exciting, and it changed too rapidly. But at an elementary class for string players I was able to write down the phrases in Ex. 63 that were repeated throughout the whole lesson, day after day:

Ex. 63

'That is "Jhinjhoti"', they told me. Another string teacher happened to be playing Jhinjhoti during that same week, and although the bit of his tune that I heard was not the same, it was obviously related:

Ex. 64

At a moderate speed for practising

When I asked my teachers how Exs. 63 and 64 could both be the same tune, they looked at me in dismay; but with ungrudging patience they sang me Jhinjhoti's modal scale, going up and coming down:

Ex. 65

'And then', they said, 'there are the notes that *catch* the raga', and they sang me Ex. 66:

Ex. 66

'For each raga', writes Daniélou,[1] 'there are a few very typical groups of notes from which it can at once be recognized. These form the main theme.'

This was as clear to follow as the *tropos spondeiakos* in Exs. 38–44 and the Mari formula in Exs. 29–35. And it helped to explain

[1] Ibid., p. 135.

how each performance of a raga can be an improvisation on a given pattern.

The performances I heard were still bewildering because I was still listening with European ears. The drum players' fingers seemed to be producing all the notes of the harmonic series, one after another, as if in defiance of the western writers on music who had declared that rhythm could exist independent of pitch. And when a string player followed a singer in a raga, echoing the improvised phrases, he was often several notes behind, so that at the ends of sentences the player would still be going up while the singer was already coming down, and for a while they would be moving in contrary motion. In my ignorance I was excited by this, and wondered why they had never developed these contrapuntal possibilities. But when I asked the director of the Lucknow Conservatoire about it he shook with laughter. 'Oh, we don't hear it like that at *all!*' he explained. 'It's like a horse and cart. The horse has to go in front of the cart, but they are both moving together.'

My pupils helped me to realize that they were not yet aware of the existence of contrary motion. 'Please teach us harmony', they had said, 'for we find our gramophone records of Beethoven symphonies disturbing and undisciplined.' Knowing that isolated notes were no use to them, I began our harmony lessons with a short, easy round for four voices. It was meant to be a humming round, but we sang it fortissimo to the Indian names of the notes:

Ex. 67[1]

It was a struggle to get it in parts, but we managed it in the end. Their eyes grew round with astonishment when they found themselves singing in harmony: they clenched their teeth and stiffened their jaws in their attempts to outsing each other, and

[1] *Singing for Pleasure,* ed. Imogen Holst, Oxford University Press, London, 1957.

they carved their way from one interval to the next with a passionate and triumphant fervour.

But if my pupils found it difficult to hear chords, I found it equally difficult *not* to hear them, especially in the modes with augmented seconds, such as the Bhairava mode in Ex. 68. (The square D flat is flatter than our tempered note, but not as flat as the lowest of the four Indian D flats.)

Ex. 68

When the singer put accents to the D flat and A flat, as in Ex. 69, the tense relation with the perpetually plucked Sa of the tampura suggested the pull of one chord against another:

Ex. 69[1]

And when he improvised in rapidly fluttering fifths and octaves (Ex. 70), the unwanted chords came nearer:

Ex. 70

While trying to banish every suggestion of harmony from the raga, I suddenly remembered the tune in the Scherzo of my father's *Choral Symphony* (Ex. 71) and realized that thanks to Bhairava I was thinking of it, for the first time, as a purely melodic line:

[1] Daniélou, op. cit., vol. II, Halcyon Press, Barnet, 1954.

Ex. 71

The Bhairava singer was Pandit Thakore of Benares, one of the great musicians of India. He looked extraordinarily like Bach, with the same full lips and high forehead as in the Haussmann portrait, and with silver-white ringlets hanging to his shoulders and a close-fitting black tunic that was half Persian and half ecclesiastical. I was allowed to sit with his elementary students while he taught them the expression of the raga called Hindola. The Hindola scale is C E F sharp A B C, and Pandit Thakore gave us the descending pattern in Ex. 72 as the kernel of the mode. (The diamond-shaped notes are slightly sharper than in the Bileval scale on page 52.)

Ex. 72

These must have been the all-important notes that my San-tiniketan friends had told me were to 'catch' the raga. Pandit Thakore kept us at them for the whole morning. He used tradi-tional hand signs while teaching us, drawing the shape of the tune in the air as he sang it, and then moulding it even more em-phatically when we tried to sing it back to him. At each repetition he grew more passionate in his appeal to us to sing it the right way. He would thrust his right hand towards the far corner of the ceiling and then drag it diagonally downwards, leaning to-wards us and offering us the completed phrase in both his hands, as if imploring us to receive it from him. At the end of the lesson he sang us the Hindola theme and the beginning of a variation. I was unable to write any of it down, for I found it impossible to take my eyes off him. But Daniélou[1] has noted the Benares tradition of this raga as it is played on the vina; Ex. 73 is the rupa, or theme, and Ex. 74 is the sthayi which establishes the theme:

Ex. 73

Ex. 74

Exs. 73 and 74 are only the beginning of a raga that might well have lasted for two hours or more. According to one of the Sanskrit textbooks, there are 490,000,000 melodic figures waiting to be used in the development of the ragas. And Pandit Thakore sounded as if he could have used them all. With so much energy and skill and invention, he seemed able to go on for ever, drawing out a wealth of long and infinitely varied melodic lines from the same small handful of notes.

[1] Daniélou, op. cit., vol. II.

CHAPTER V

The 'Cantus Firmus'

'The Orient', says Sachs,[1] 'has kept alive melodic styles that mediaeval Europe choked to death under the hold of harmony.' The words are violent, but they are true. As soon as the excitement of the 'harmony' of counterpoint took hold of the minds of mediaeval musicians there was no longer any opportunity for elaborate improvisation in the style of the *Jubilate* in Ex. 50.

The first singers to break away from the pure melodic line of plainchant can hardly be called discoverers, for the sounds they produced were an aberration rather than an invention.

There is little to choose between the parallel fourths and fifths of ninth-century Europe and the instinctive 'organum' of twentieth-century Africa:

Ex. 75[2]

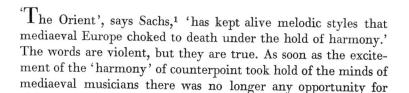

In his book on African music, A. M. Jones says that 'many tribes

---

[1] Sachs, op. cit., p. 29.

[2] A. M. Jones, *Studies in African Music*, Oxford University Press, London, 1959, vol. II, p. 139.

. . . sing the bulk of a chorus in unison, only breaking into fourths at certain places. . . . These Africans carry in their minds the notion that a fourth below any given note is an equivalent of, or at least an alternative to, that note, and can be used as an embellishment and by way of a change when repeating a melody [i.e. tune]. When he drops to this note the singer is *thinking* in terms of the original melody. Thus the note a fourth below is really an alternative way of conceiving the note in its true position. It *indicates* the original note.'[1]

This must also have been the feeling of the ninth-century monks. Their plainsong was able to wander up and down in fourths and fifths without discomfort, for the chants were innocent of the subtle and sensuous portamento of Indian ragas. The early Fathers of the Church had seen to this: as long ago as the second century, Clement of Alexandria was already making it clear that 'one must not expose oneself to the powerful influence of exciting and languorous modes, which by the curve of their melodies lead to effeminacy and infirmity of purpose'.[2] There was nothing in the plain outline of the *Tonus Peregrinus* that prevented it from being sung in fifths:

Ex. 76[3]

When this is doubled at the octave in a resonant church or cathedral, the sound is magnificent. But the movement is not potent enough to be called 'harmony'.

In its artlessness, this instinctive parallelism might easily have

[1] Jones, op. cit., vol. I, p. 241.
[2] Quoted in *The Pelican History of Music*, Penguin Books, Harmondsworth, 1960, vol. I, p. 147.
[3] O. Strunk, *Source Readings in Music History*, Faber & Faber, London, 1952.

lived an unpretentious life of its own in secluded parish churches, remaining on the fringe of literacy, like the parallel fifths in Icelandic folk songs that were still being published in students' song-books in the mid-nineteenth century. Organum, however, was bound to emerge as a scholarly pursuit, because the musicians of the late ninth century were insatiable theorists. In their *Scholia Enchiriadis* of about 900 they wrote *Nos qui vivimus* in every possible position of parallel fourths and fifths and octaves, describing the different blendings as 'Symphonies'. In the text of the *Enchiriadis*, which is in the usual form of a dialogue between master and pupil, the master explains, with diagrams, why octaves, fifths and fourths are able to respond consonantly to one another. 'There is equal sound at the octave because sounds are here brought together by duple relationship (as 6 to 12). At the fifth, sounds respond consonantly because they are in the ratio 6 to 9, . . . and at the fourth . . . 6 to 8.'[1]

At this point the pupil says: 'I perceive clearly that Arithmetic is necessary to an understanding of Music.' 'Absolutely necessary,' replies the master, 'for music is fashioned wholly in the likeness of numbers.'

The master demonstrates that, at the interval of a fourth, organum does not remain strictly parallel, because 'by a certain natural law of its own it stands still in certain places and is unable to proceed further':

Ex. 77[2]

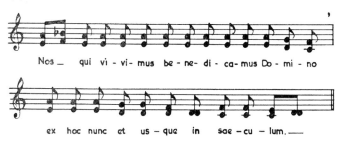

Nos — qui vi - vi- mus be - ne- di - ca- mus Do - mi - no

ex hoc nunc et us – que in sae – cu – lum. —

'Why?' asks the pupil, with admirable insistence. The master makes him sing four rising notes, first on A B C D, and then at

---

[1] Ibid., p. 136.
[2] Ibid.

61

the different levels of G A B C, F G A B and E F G A. And the pupil realizes that a parallel *vox organalis* in Ex. 77 would go outside the mode, which is why the Africans came together on a unison in Ex. 75, and the Mari singers altered the shape of their answer in Ex. 30.

The forcible theft of that last bit of the tune in Ex. 77 marks the beginning of eleven hundred years of organized distortion.

The freely-flowing rhythm of a *jubilus* was already threatened, even before organum, by the mediaeval churchman's habit of writing syllabic words to fit melismatic tunes, as in Ex. 79:

Ex. 78

Ex. 79[1]

The legato of Ex. 79 is endangered, but not destroyed. In Exs. 76 and 77, however, the organum has increased the danger by tempting the singers to dig down into their stressed syllables in order to keep together. (This is a danger the African singers are not aware of in Ex. 75: their dance is in measured rhythm, appearing in Jones's transcription as three-eight duplets against five different percussive cross-rhythms that are linked by the silent hand-clap in the background.)

Plainsong must also have suffered a distortion in the pitch of several of its melodic intervals when it allowed itself to be sung in parallel fourths and fifths. This is a loss we seldom worry about in our present equal-tempered existence. It was my Indian pupils who first made me realize it. I had tried to get them to sing organum at the fourth, dividing them into two groups and asking

[1] *Harvard Anthology of Music*, ed. A. T. Davison and W. Apel.

one group to sing the tune C-D-E while the others sang F-G-A. The journey from C and F to D and G was successful, but when we got to the next step they broke off with a shuddering protest. 'We can't go on,' they said. 'You forget that the distance from Ri to Ga is smaller than from Pa to Dha.' (See page 52.) They shook their heads sadly and glanced away, as if I had brought them to the verge of some frightful indiscretion. We left it at that, and gave up all attempts to sing organum. But they were never able to understand how western musicians could say that C and D or D and E were 'a tone apart', without also mentioning that C–D was a larger tone than D–E.

The distortions in pitch in ninth-century parallel organum, however, were negligible compared with the rhythmical havoc caused by twelfth-century independent part-writing. The long-drawn-out breves in Ex. 80 are barely recognizable as the same chant as Ex. 78: the tune has sacrificed its original meaning in order to become a *cantus firmus*. In Ex. 80, the *Kyrie* is not only 'fixed' in the sense of 'prescribed', it has also become firm and solid:

Ex. 80[1]

It is impossible to imagine the state of mind of the twelfth-century Spanish tenor who first sang the upper part in Ex. 80. We cannot even be sure how he fitted his freely-flowing melismas to the augmentation of the *Cantus*. It must have been easier for the singers to listen vertically when they approached their intervals, or 'symphonies', with the deliberate attack of measured rhythm:

[1] Adapted from *Harvard Anthology*.

Ex. 81[1]

By the time Léonin wrote this Alleluia he was already near the end of his great book of two-part organa for Notre Dame, and he could balance his phrases with the skill of long experience. The two voices are linked in a tenuous outline of parallel octaves and fifths, yet the upper voice has an individual tune of its own and can thoroughly enjoy the independent rhythm that allows it to end a phrase halfway through bar 9, at the very moment when the augmentation is attacking the beginning of a new note. It is these changes of level in the long-held bass notes that must have been difficult to organize in the earliest experiments in two-part writing: they need the courageous imagination of a mind that is not content with vertical symphonies but is already thinking with the continuity of what we call harmony. The first five bars of Ex. 81 could easily have been sung by a primitive folk singer, moving between tonic and dominant over the drone of a bagpipe. But the sudden shift of the drone in the sixth bar would have silenced the bagpiper, just as it would have defeated my Indian pupils in Santiniketan. The level of their own Indian Sa was movable: they could choose any convenient pitch for tuning the drone of the tampura. But once the level had been decided on, they kept to it for the whole session of two or three hours. When they first asked me to play them English folk dances on the recorder, I began by choosing a different key for each tune, with

[1] W. G. Waite, *The Rhythm of Twelfth-Century Polyphony*, Yale, 1954.

carefully planned key relations running through the whole group, just as if it had been a programme for a European concert. But they implored me to keep to the same tonic for every tune, because they found it impossible to adjust themselves so quickly to the imagined sound of a new drone.

The courage of the twelfth-century composers reached its triumphant climax when Léonin's successor Pérotin began writing for as many as four voices:

Ex. 82[1]

from Viderunt

Pérotin

etc.

[1] B.M., Egerton MS 2615.

E

To the eye of the twentieth-century reader who has never lived with these sounds, the time-patterns may appear to have borrowed too much from the naïve repetitions of a Trouvère's song such as Ex. 83:

Ex. 83[1]

Le Tournoiement des Dames   Huon d'Oisy (12th.cent.)

Et l'an que che-va-lier sont   A-bau-bi,   Ke d'armes noi-
                                        Lez da-mez tour-

-ent ne font · Li har-di,   Le tour-noi-e-ment ple-vi,
-noi-er vont A Lai-gni.

La con-tes-se de Cres-pi   Di-ent que sa-voir vou-drant Quel
Et ma-da-me de Cou-ci   Lez da-mez par tout le mont Pour

li colp sont, Que pour e-les font Lour a-mi.   Y-o-lenz—
-cha-cier font Qu'e-lez men-ront Chas-cune od li.   Mar-ge-ri - -

de Cail-li   Vait pre-mierz—   as-sam-bler;
-te d'Oy-si   Muet a li—   pour jous-ter.

Here the tune thrives on its cheerful repetition, and the skipping syllables are as welcome as in a children's singing game. But the rhythm of Pérotin's *Viderunt* inhabits a different world. In the vast resonance of Notre Dame, between the pedal-point of a mediaeval organ and the fluctuating overtones of suspended hand-bells, the intervals would have needed time to make themselves heard. In appearance, the modern twelve-eight seems deceptively like a pastorale, but in sound it is much more emphatic. The quavers are not passing-notes: they are deliberate changes of

[1] *New Oxford History of Music*, vol. II, p. 233.

level in the vertical structure. The singers of 1198 must have carved their way from one interval to the next with the same stiff-jawed determination that my Indian friends showed when they were faced with the first four-part harmony they had ever met.

The weighty emphasis is needed, for *Viderunt* is built on a massive scale. The extended organum, lasting for twenty-five minutes, is an astonishing achievement, and the sound is glorious from beginning to end. But there is no disguising the fact that the relentlessly measured in-and-out of the part-writing has choked to death the subtle twists and turns of plainsong. As for the *cantus firmus*, it has become so fixed that it is almost inanimate: the first two syllables of the word 'Viderunt' last for over three minutes before the F moves up to A.

Pérotin's earlier *Beata viscera*, written for a single voice, still enjoys the flowing freedom that had to be sacrificed in *Viderunt*:

Ex. 84[1]

from Beata viscera   Pérotin

O _____ mi – – ra no – – vi –

– tas et no – vum gau-di – – um, Ma – tris in – te – – gri –

– tas post – – – – – pu-er-pe – – ri – – um

And in Ex. 85 the solitary singer can allow the clear lines of his hymn to float off into a lightly-graced melisma at each cadence, as in the 'reiterative' cadences of plainsong:

[1] *Harvard Anthology*, p. 14. The editors say that their rhythmic interpretation is meant to bring out the peculiar mixture of metrical and non-metrical elements in the tune.

Ex. 85[1]

It took nearly three hundred years for polyphonic tunes to become as flowing and gracious as the plainsong tunes on which they were founded. In Ex. 86 Dunstable's variant for the second verse of *Ave maris Stella* is a fitting alternative to the plainsong:

Ex. 86

---

[1] Ibid., p. 15.
[2] John Dunstable, *Complete Works*, ed. M. F. Bukofzer, Royal Musical Association (Stainer & Bell, London).

In Ex. 88[1] the flowing lines are just as gracious as in Ex. 86, but it is another kind of beauty, and in order to achieve it, the composer has mutilated the plainsong of Ex. 87, dividing it among the various voices, so that the listener is compelled to follow the music obliquely.

In this polyphonic texture the listener, while being aware that the soprano is singing a variant of the complete tune, is also able to hear that the first four notes have been lopped off, and that they have gained a new lease of life by being sung in canonic imitation by one voice after another, over and over again, at alternating levels of pitch. (In the 1521 edition the words *qui perseveraverit salvus erit*—'he who perseveres shall be saved'—are printed above the notes of the ostinato, giving a vivid glimpse of the working of a mediaeval composer's mind.)

[1] Ed. H. T. David, Music Press, New York, 1947.

Ex. 87

Sal - - ve Re - - gi - - - - na

Ex. 88

Josquin

Of all the ways in which a tune can adapt itself to circumstances, this oblique continuity is surely the most astonishing. A whole tune can be claimed at different times by any number of different voices and yet remain clear as in Exs. 89 and 90:

Ex. 89[1]

[1] *Collected Vocal Works of William Byrd*, ed. E. H. Fellowes, Stainer & Bell.

Ex. 90[1]

Weelkes

[1] B.M. Add. MSS 17786–91.

This piling up of the entries is the polyphonic equivalent of the reiterative cadences in plainsong: the voices tread as closely as in those renaissance pictures where the angels are crowding into the courts of heaven, leaving each other scarcely any room to play their instruments.

The crowding of the voices in Ex. 90 has led to an apparent discrepancy in bar 10, where the first tenor's 'in excelsis' arrives off the beat. But the beat is not a beat. It is as inaudible as an Indian or African handclap.

There is room for any amount of fluid cross-rhythm in sixteenth-century polyphony. In Ex. 91 each singer follows the rhythm of his own version of the tune, whether it is in twos or threes, without disturbing the freedom of the effortless legato:

Ex. 91[1]

When the words themselves are accumulative, the close entries can have a startlingly dramatic effect, as in the building up of 'we praise thee, we bless thee', in Ex. 92:

[1] Fitzwilliam MS 88/122.

Ex. 92[1]

from Missa sine nomine   Taverner

[1] Adapted from *Tudor Church Music*, ed. E. H. Fellowes, vol. I, Oxford University Press, London, 1923.

The simple dance-like rhythm of the unanimous *Gratias* comes as a relief to the singers, after the exciting rhythms of the close imitation. For the vitality of the greatest polyphonic music is too overwhelming to be kept up for long at a stretch.

Listeners also find it a relief to meet a tune that can float unimpaired on the surface of the harmony. Elaborate polyphony is
easier to sing than to listen to, for there are subtleties that can
only be fully enjoyed from inside the music. Even the sixteenth-
century listeners complained that there were tunes that 'pierce
not, but without leaving any taste of themselves, pass by the ears
not accustomed to hear them'.[1]

And even the composers, at the height of their polyphonic
splendour, began to turn to a 'first singing part' for the tune.
Byrd's 1588 set of 'Psalms, Sonnets and Songs' was originally
'made for Instruments to expresse the harmonie, and one voyce
to pronounce the dittie'. And in Morley's five-part Canzonets of
1597, the *cantus* becomes a tune in its own right, that can be
taken away and sung in solitude:

 Ex. 93[2]

At the beginning of this volume of canzonets Morley writes a
letter of dedication to his patron, saying: 'I have also set them
tablature-wise to the lute in the Cantus book for one to sing and
play alone when your Lordship would retire yourself and be more

[1] B. Castiglione, trans. Sir Thomas Hoby, 1561. Quoted in Strunk, op. cit.
[2] *English Madrigal School*, ed. E. H. Fellowes, Stainer & Bell, vol. III.

private.' English amateurs were beginning to agree with the Italians that although madrigal singing might be 'a fair music, . . . to sing to the lute is much better because all the sweetness consisteth in one alone . . . and a man is much more heedful and understandeth better . . . the air or vein of it when the ears are not busied in hearing any more than one voice'.[1]

[1] Castiglione, op. cit.

CHAPTER VI

Songs to the Lute

'The musik must be of itself exquisite, but in the manner, as comon as the high way; otherwise they will say, Wee do not understand this.' Roger North was trying to answer his own question, 'What is Ayre?', and at the end of his essay he had to admit that 'as for securing an Ayre, . . . it is like securing witt in poetry, not to be done; and after all will be found to flow from a genius, and not without some accidents or rather felicitys of fancy, as well as sound judgment, to make it sublime.'[1]

The geniuses who wrote the English lutenist songs made their music sound deceptively simple: Campian's tune for 'The peaceful western wind' could almost be mistaken for a folk song:

Ex. 94[2]

The peace-ful west-ern wind The win-ter's storms hath tamed; And Na-ture in each kind The kind heat hath in-flamed. The for-ward buds so sweet-ly breathe Out of their earth-y bowers, That heav'n, which views their pomp be-neath Would fain be deck'd with flowers.

---

[1] *Roger North on Music*, pp. 69 and 92.
[2] Examples 94–104 are taken from *The English School of Lutenist Song Writers*, ed. E. H. Fellowes, Stainer & Bell.

The manner is 'as common as the highway', but it is not the language of folk song. The first half of the tune hints at an open-air simplicity, but the second half ventures beyond the control of the mode and is influenced by harmony. The line about the earthy bowers could never have grown into that shape without the encouragement of modulation. And the words, for all their enchantment, sound as if they have been reared with a bookish deliberation. They take delight in the pun on 'kind', and prefer to look at the pomp of spring from a different level than that of the traditional folk song.

When Campian chose to write a mock folk tune he did it whole-heartedly:

Ex. 95   Campian

Campian's songs are 'artificial' in the true sixteenth-century meaning of the word. 'In these English Ayres', he told his readers, 'I have chiefly aymed to couple my Words and Notes lovingly together, which will be much for him to doe that hath not power over both.'

He himself was equally at home with words and music, and when he set out to write his verses he may already have had the tunes lurking in the back of his mind. But it was not only the poet-composers who made their songs sound as if the words and the music had grown up together. In Rosseter's tunes to Campian's poems the two are linked just as faithfully:

Ex. 96

(Words by Campian)   Rosseter

Whe-ther men do laugh or weep, Whe-ther they do wake or sleep,

Whe-ther they die young or old, Whe-ther they feel heat or cold,

There is un-der-neath the sun No-thing in true ear-nest done.

It is house-music, to be heard casually after a meal. The singer can drop his voice to a confidential whisper if he wishes to, for he will never be faced with the street-crier's problem of having to deal with the consonants in 'Brushes and brooms' on a long-held fortissimo. He can welcome all the consonants that he meets, using their energy to draw out the rhythm of the tune as well as the meaning of the words.

Campian discouraged long melismas, insisting that 'we ought to maintaine in Nature as in action a manly cariage, gracing no word but that which is eminent and emphaticall'.

It is this occasional gracing of nouns and verbs within the framework of a syllabic phrase that gives Ex. 97 its satisfying shape:

Ex. 97

Rosseter

When Lau-ra smiles,___ her sight re-vives___ both night and day;   etc.
The earth and heav'n ___ views with de - light ___ her wan-ton play;

According to Campian, 'English stands chiefly upon mona-sillables'. He might well have gone on to say that many of them are so onomatopoeic that they are almost crying out to be set to music.

The lutenist song-writers had no need to analyse the words they were using. When Campian attempted it in his *Observations in the Art of English Poesie* he became entangled with the difference between accent and quantity, and he poured scorn on the 'foolish figurative repetition' which he used so magically in his verses. He never once mentioned the riches of onomatopoeia, for they could be taken for granted.

It was in the seventeenth and eighteenth centuries that poets brought their inquiring minds to the 'great agreement' in their native tongue 'between the sounds of the letters and the thing signified'. Doctor Johnson devotes several pages of his *Dictionary* to quotations from Wallis's examples of onomatopoeia which he thought were sufficiently ingenious to be included, though with characteristic caution he warns his readers that they are 'of more subtlety than solidity'.

'Words that begin with *str*', writes Wallis, 'intimate force . . . as *strong, strike, strive, stretch* . . .

'*St* in like manner implies strength, but in less degree, denoting something firm and fixed, as *stand, stay, stick, step, stamp*.

'*Thr* implies a more violent degree of motion, as *throw, thrust, threaten*.

'*Wr* implies some sort of distortion, as *wrest, wring, wrong, wrench* . . .

'*Sw* implies a silent agitation or a softer kind of motion, as *sway, swerve, sweep, swim*. Nor is there much difference of *sm* in *smooth, smile*.

'*Cl* denotes a kind of adhesion or tenacity, as in *cling, climb, clasp, close*.

'*Sp* implies an expansion, especially a quick one, particularly if there be an *r*; for example, *spread, spring, sprout*.

'*Sl* is a kind of silent fall, or a less observable motion, as in *slide, slip, slow, slack*. [He forgets to mention *sleep*.]

'*Ash*, as acting more nimbly and sharply: *crash, flash, clash*.

'But *ush*, as acting more obtusely and dully: *crush, brush, hush.* Yet in both there is a swift and sudden motion, not instantaneous, but gradual, by the continued sound *sh*.

'In *fling, sing, wring, sting*, the tingling of the termination *ng* implies the continuation of a very slender motion or tremour, at length indeed vanishing, but not suddenly interrupted.

'In *wink, sink, clink* . . . there is a sudden ending.

'If there be an *l* as in *jingle, mingle, sprinkle, twinkle*, there is implied frequency or iteration of small acts. And the same frequency, but less subtle by reason of the clearer vowel *a*, is indicated in *jangle, wrangle, dangle*: also in *mumble, stumble, crumble, fumble*, but the close *u* implies something obscure . . . and a congeries of consonants, *mble*, denotes a confused kind of rolling or tumbling. . . .

'In *sparkle, sp* denotes dissipation, *ar* an acute crackling, *k* a sudden interruption, *l* a frequent iteration. In like manner, in *squeak, crack, hisse, whirl, buz, twist* and in many more, we may observe the agreement of such sort of sounds with the things signified: and this so frequently happens, that scarce any language which I know can be compared with ours.'

Singing exaggerates the possibilities of onomatopoeia, making the sounds even more potent. And the potency helps to build tunes. It is the physical shaping of the sung words 'laugh or weep', 'wake or sleep' that shapes the tune in Ex. 96, with its relaxed falling quavers for the wide-open laugh before the sudden drawing together of the lips for the modulation of 'weep', and with its lively 'k' in 'wake' cutting a sharp edge to the crotchets before reaching the 'silent fall' of 'sleep'.

The singable quality of 'l', 'm' and 'n' makes it possible for the twelve-syllabled phrase of 'The peaceful western wind' (Ex. 94) to flow in an unbroken stream of sound with a gentle rise and fall that is nearly as smooth as a plainsong melisma.

The singer's staccato at the 't' and 'd' in 'I care not for those Ladies' (Ex. 95) gives the six-eight tune the persuasive lift of tongued quavers in an instrumental dance. And the scornful tone of voice at the word 'pray'd' is stretched to the very edge of absurdity by the singer's exaggerated 'r' which carries the note along with it as it rolls.

The alliteration in the spoken verse of Ex. 98 becomes even livelier when sung:

Ex. 98

The rolled 'r' furrows its way through 'Frowns print wrinkles in thy brows', with the pattern of the vowels reflected in the pattern of the tune. And the quick expansion of the 'sp' in 'spiteful' comes as near to spitting as it dares, before the muscles draw inwards for their thin-lipped 'smile'.

It is not only in the expressive sound of their words that the poems come more than halfway to meet the composer: they also offer him phrases that carry their own gesture with them. In 'Shall I sue? Shall I seek for grace?' (Ex. 99) the line that strives to a heavenly joy is balanced in the poem by the line that ascends the clouds, just when Dowland is needing another curving arch to his tune:

Ex. 99

Shall I think that a bleed-ing heart Or a wound-ed eye,

Or a sigh can as-cend the clouds To at-tain so high?

The restlessness of the opening lines in Ex. 99, with the swift 'sh' pushing each question forward, is in perfect contrast to the languishing six-eight of the 'wounded eye'. This changeable hemiolia, which is borrowed from the patterns of mediaeval counterpoint, is a rhythm that frequently finds its way into the lutenist songs: in the flowing four-four of 'Come, Phyllis' (Ex. 100) it brings a sudden marcato to the gesture of the words, as if the singer were deliberately pointing at each chirping bird:

Ex. 100

Ford

Come Phyllis, come in-to these bowers; Here shel-ter is from

sharp-est showers. Cool gales of wind breathe in these shades,

Dan-ger none this place in-vades. Here sit, and note the

chirp-ing birds Plead-ing my love, plead-ing my

love in si - lent _____ words.

At the end of the verse, the gesture of pleading stretches the tune beyond the spoken length of the line: the closely-bound words and music begin to pull apart. It is a sign of the inevitable distortion that happens when a poem is turned into music. In *A History of Song*,[1] Michael Tippett goes so far as to say that 'the music of a song destroys the verbal music of the poem utterly'. The statement comes as a shock and sounds like a flagrant exaggeration. But even the lutenists often distorted the metrical rhythm of the verses they were setting.

Generations of readers of Campian's poems have enjoyed the verbal music of 'If she forsake me' without knowing the sound of its tune:

> *If she forsake me, I must die;*
> *Shall I tell her so?*
> *Alas, then straight will she reply*
> *No, no, no, no, no.*
> *If I disclose my desperate state,*
> *She will but make sport thereat*
> *And more unrelenting grow.*
>
> *I do my love in lines commend,*
> *But alas in vain,*
> *The costly gifts that I do send*
> *She returns again.*
> *Thus still is my despair procured,*
> *And her malice more assured.*
> *Then come, death, and end my pain.*

Rosseter's tune to 'If she forsake me' scatters this verbal rhythm and sends it flying with its swift plunge into diminution:

Ex. 101

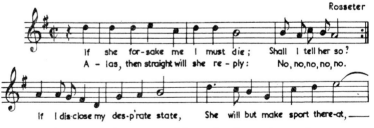

[1] Ed. Denis Stevens, Hutchinson, London, 1960, p. 462.

86

When sung to its tune, the last line, 'Then come, death, and
end my pain', reaches a delicate irony that belongs to the world
of *Così fan tutte*. The same irony can be heard in 'Beauty is but
a painted hell', where the passionately explosive labials give way
to the sighing cadence of 'Ay me':

Ex. 102

The singer cannot convey the full expression of these last two
bars without the lute, for the sighing exclamations need their
chords. In their artificial simplicity the tunes may seem at first
to be self-sufficient, but they are incomplete without the sound
of their harmonies: the 'dull notes', as Campian called them,
need discords 'for helps to grace them'. And, of all instruments,
the lute is the best suited for the gracing. It is the perfect partner
to the voice, supporting syncopations, building up a crescendo
and sustaining the energy of a long-held word:

Ex. 103

The lute, according to sixteenth-century listeners, added to the words 'such a grace and strength' that it was 'a great wonder'. The player's finger-tips could produce subtle variations of attack that rivalled the singer's expressive consonants. The furrows of 'frowns print wrinkles' in Ex. 98 are more relentless when the lute draws them with a fierce marcato. In the 'sharpest showers' of Ex. 100, the stroking of the strings sends a scudding splash of sound into the air. And in 'Beauty is but a painted hell' (Ex. 102) the snap of the string bites at the finger with a vicious impetus.

There are no native monosyllables that the lute cannot reinforce with its own wordless onomatopoeia. When the singer sighs, the lute sighs with him, letting the sound float into silence. The capacity for sighing is a legacy from the lute's oriental ancestors: according to Picken,[1] the seven-stringed Chinese zither was used 'to suggest, rather than to produce sounds'. Another legacy from the East is the lute's portamento which can colour a word such as 'cling', underlining the tenacity of the *cl* by the pressure of a microtonal slide, and sharing the tingling of the *ng* by supporting the singer's 'tremour' with a fingered vibrato.

These are the subtleties of expression that Dowland had at his own finger-tips when he sang and played his songs to the lute. In his genius for summoning darkness and despair he could transform the lyrics into passionate monologues:

Ex. 104

[1] *New Oxford History of Music*, vol. I, p. 87.

In this final sentence of 'Sorrow, stay', the air is becoming extended into an aria and the music is already moving towards the language of Purcell. But, as Tippett has pointed out,[1] 'Dowland's is basically private grief, and Purcell's is public and theatrical.'

'Sorrow, stay' was perhaps one of the last of the sad sixteenth-century songs to be sung under an open window or in the alcove of a room, with the sigh of the lute's strings melting into silence. Grief, elsewhere, was already being presented in sung declamation on the operatic stage.

[1] *Henry Purcell: Essays on his Music,* ed. Imogen Holst, Oxford University Press, London, 1959, p. 46.

CHAPTER VII

The 'Stile Rappresentativo'

———— ❧ ————

It was during the fifteen-eighties that Count Bardi began inviting poets and musicians to his palace in Florence to meet the rich amateurs who were his friends, and to join in the discussions on 'how to improve modern music and raise it in some degree from the wretched state to which it had been reduced'.[1] They had chosen the moment when music was at the height of what is now described as its Golden Age. But Bardi's 'Camerata' had little use for polyphony. They complained that the sole aim of counterpoint was to delight the ear. They insisted that it was impossible for a singer to pronounce his words intelligibly if the composer had been 'carried away' by canonic imitation. And they were shocked to find that the contrapuntists had 'not a book among them for their use' that would show them how to express 'the conceptions of the mind'.[2]

These reformers of sixteenth-century music were not setting out to invent opera: they were trying to discover what sort of music the Greek dramatists had used in their performances. Someone had told them that the tragedies were sung from beginning to end, and they were determined to revive this noble style of presentation. There were no ancient Greek tunes for them to sing: the few fragments of Greek music we now possess had not yet been deciphered. But there were a great many theoretical works for them to study, including several that must have proved gloomy reading. There was Aristotle's discussion on 'whether we are to prefer music with a good melody or music with a good

[1] Strunk, op. cit., p. 364.
[2] Ibid., p. 312.

91

rhythm', and his discouraging question: 'Why need people learn to perform themselves instead of enjoying music played by others?'—a question that must have sounded odd to those highly intelligent amateurs of 1580, who played the lute and sang madrigals as a relaxation and did a little composing in their spare time. But they persevered with their reading, for they were obsessed with the idea of finding out what kind of song Timotheus had sung when he roused Alexander to combat with the armies of his foes. They decided that the aim of the ancient music was to 'induce in another the same passion that one feels oneself',[1] and they asked young composers to go to the theatre and to notice how the actors changed their speech from high to low, and from quick to slow, and how loud their voices were in tragedies or comedies, and what sort of gestures they used while declaiming their lines.

This was the advice that led to recitative, which Dryden was to define as 'a kind of tuneful pronunciation, more musical than common speech, and less than song'.

Peri has described[2] how he set to work to provide sung declamation to Rinuccini's texts for the Camerata's productions: 'In thinking of the problem of imitating speech in music, I realized that some words in our language hold a sound that can be used as a basis for harmony, and that during a conversation one passes through many other words which are not so singable, before again reaching one which can lead to a new consonance. And thinking of the many changes of inflexion and accent which show grief, joy and so on, I made the bass move with them. And I held firmly to the same bass note through discords and concords, until the voice of the declaimer, after running through various quick notes, arrived once more at a word that was singable in ordinary speech, and this opened the way to a new harmony.'

The new style had an immediate success. The Italian language, with its sonorous open vowels, seemed naturally adapted to recitative. Listeners were impressed; they felt that this was indeed how the gods would have spoken on Olympus or in the Elysian shades, with a dignity suitable to their character.

Recitative gave the singers an opportunity for expressive rubato,

[1] Ibid., p. 317.
[2] Angelo Solerti, *Le origini del melodramma*, Turin, 1903.

and having been built on a firm foundation of chords, it allowed them the emotional luxury of augmented or diminished intervals:

Ex. 105[1]

This 'dashing upon harsh notes' must have made a vivid impression after the mainly step-wise tunes of polyphony. But expressive intervals were not enough to turn Peri's recitatives into real melodies, and the first performance of his *Euridice* would not have had such a success without the arias by his rival composer Caccini, who happened to be better at writing tunes than recitatives.

The music of *Euridice* is seldom revived, but Caccini's arias are still sung, and there can be few twentieth-century singing pupils venturing on the first rung of *bel canto* who have not at some time or other practised his 'Amarilli, mia bella':

Ex. 106

[1] *Harvard Anthology*, vol. II.

The tune would not have sounded in the least like Ex. 106 during Caccini's lifetime. Not only would the figured bass have been realized with 'the inner voices played on an instrument to express the passion of the words', but the tune itself would have been so graced with embellishments that its outline would have been scarcely recognizable.

In his *Nuove Musiche* of 1601, Caccini has left detailed instructions for the interpretation of graces and ornaments and trills, and has given hints on how to provide the right rubato for each 'exclamation'. 'I have endeavoured', he says in Playford's translation,[1] 'to bring in a kind of Musick, by which men might as it were Talk in Harmony, using in that kind of Singing a certain noble neglect of the Song (as I have heard at *Florence* by the Actors in their Singing *Opera's*) in which I have endeavoured the Imitation of the Conceit of the Words, seeking out the Cords more or less passionate, according to the meaning of them.' Ex. 107 shows how elaborately he graced the final cadence of a love song:

Ex. 107[2]

---

[1] J. Playford, *Introduction to the Skill of Musick*, 1674 edition, p. 37.
[2] *Harvard Anthology*, vol. II.

The rapidly repeated notes of the *trillo* needed a new kind of technique, for the mediaeval tremolo had been forgotten during the centuries of polyphonic singing. It was still used in traditional calls when herdsmen had to make their voices carry for a great distance in the open air. But the sophisticated singers of the seventeenth century had to practise the 'beating of the throat' as a technical exercise, and Playford was delighted when he found that a young English singer had learnt the Caccini *trillo* by 'imitating that breaking of a sound in the throat which men use when they lure their hawks, as *he-he-he-he-he*'.

The beating of the throat in the dotted rhythm of Ex. 107 is elaborate enough to have been borrowed from an improvised variation in a raga. But although the time-patterns might be appropriate in Indian singing, the melodic line is in an entirely different language, for each rise and fall is shaped by the changing harmony of the bass line.

There was nothing new about listening vertically and building up a melodic line from the harmonies suggested by the bass notes. Campian, at the time when he was writing his lute songs, was already aware that 'the Base containes in it both the Aire and the true judgement of the Key'. The new discovery in the Caccini arias was the wealth of expression that ornamentation could bring to the words of a song. It was just what was wanted in the *stile rappresentativo*, to relieve the pages of recitative where the music had to follow the laws of speech. A simple unadorned air, with a tune like a folk song, would have been of no use in a Florentine opera, for it would have made the recitatives seem out of place and 'theatrical' in the wrong sense of the word. In *The Beggar's Opera* the tunes always sound welcome because they stand out clearly and triumphantly from the spoken dialogue that surrounds them: they can afford to be as compact and self-supporting as they choose. But the music of real opera needs to be theatrical, in the true sense, from beginning to end, if the representation is to be convincing. Airs must become arias, and tunes have to turn into melodies.

The Camerata composers were ruthless enough to achieve the necessary transformation. They took time over their non-realistic arias, and got on with the story in their quasi-realistic recitatives. And as a result they invented opera.

They were also responsible for bringing into existence a good deal of the operatic paraphernalia that we are now familiar with. From the very beginning there were the rivalries: Caccini rushing into print in 1600 with *his* version of Rinuccini's *Euridice*, in order to get it out a few months before Peri, and Peri explaining in public that *his* version had been composed first, and that it had been presented before Her Most Christian Majesty and received with universal applause; the only reason why Caccini had composed some of the arias for this performance being 'because they were to be sung by persons under his direction, who were dependent on him'.

There are descriptions of Count Bardi 'toiling night after night in the arduous venture' (did the rich amateurs copy out the parts?), and descriptions of how the singers wasted time at rehearsals by telling everyone about their sore throats and their stomach troubles and their sleepless nights.[1]

Eight years after this first performance Rinuccini was writing *Arianne* and *Il ballo delle ingrate* for Monteverdi in Mantua. Opera had come to stay.

Monteverdi already knew that the words he was setting had to rule the music, and no one could teach him anything about 'imitating their conceit'.

It is not only in his operas that his phrases are shaped like gestures: in his church music he could scatter the proud and exalt the humble with tunes that had no need of action to convey their drama:

Ex. 108[2]

from Magnificat Primo   Monteverdi
Quick
di - sper   sit sup-er-bos

[1] Solerti, op. cit.
[2] *Musica Religiosa*, II, Tomo XV, ed. Malipiero, Universal.

Ex. 109[1]

In his madrigals, Monteverdi could seize hold of a word and repeat it a dozen times with the fanatical insistence of a dog worrying a bone:

Ex. 110

Quick

This is what the foreword to his 1608 Madrigals describes as 'an attempt to depict anger in music'. But it was very much more than that. Anger was only a small part of the energy that he let loose on the language of music. He made it possible for the spoken rhythm of a word to stand out with sudden monumental significance, so that a hundred years later Bach could break in on Pilate's questioning with the savage shout of 'Barabbas!', and two hundred years later, Verdi could disturb a tense pool of silence in his *Requiem* by dropping into it his muttered 'Mors . . . Mors . . . Mors . . .'

One of the earliest of the great composers to learn this new energy from Monteverdi was Schütz. He had already touched the fringe of the Florentine tradition in his opera *Dafne*, which was founded on a libretto Rinuccini had written for the Camerata. A year after it had been performed, Schütz interrupted his work in Germany because he could not bear to miss hearing the Venetian performances of Monteverdi's latest compositions. In his own sacred songs the singer declaims his text with an actor's intensity and flings his repeated questions to the four corners of the church:

[1] Ibid.

Ex. 111

Ach, wo-hin, wo - hin, wo-hin, wo – hin, du Sohn Got - tes?

It is as insistent as Purcell's cry of 'Gabriel! Where's Gabriel?'

Purcell was born too late to have heard Monteverdi's performances, but it is good to know, as a result of recent research, that he copied out the beginning of one of Monteverdi's madrigals on the same page as his own *Benedicite*.

Purcell also knew of the Camerata, for he was familiar with his friend Playford's translation of Caccini's discourse on the new music, and he had read about the trills and exclamations, and the 'noble neglect' of the song, and the Florentines' attempts to talk in harmony in their tunes.

Purcell's own 'imitations' leap up from the pages of the *Orpheus Britannicus*, even when it is opened at random:

Ex. 112

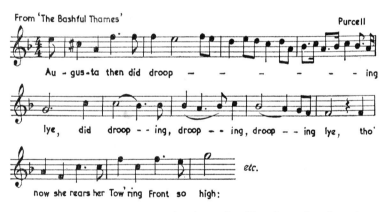

From 'The Bashful Thames'

Au – gus-ta then did droop — — — — — - ing

lye, did droop - - ing, droop - - ing, droop - - ing lye, tho'

now she rears her Tow'ring Front so high:

The 'drooping' and the 'rearing' are familiar formulas, but they are welcome at each repetition, and the vitality of the tune is irrepressible.

Another random choice, 'Wake, Quivera', shows the same tireless delight in following each gesture of 'opening' and 'falling', with the stored-up energy of syncopation urging the singer through the 'drive'. (A typically Purcellian pun, since syncopation was known as 'driving' in the seventeenth century.)

Ex. 113

From 'Wake Quivera'

'Never' is one of those words that can be repeated half a dozen times without damaging the meaning of a sentence: in Purcell's hands its rhythm can support the whole structure of a tune, varying in timing and dynamics from cheerful and triumphant to tender and tragic.

In spite of all that the historians can say, Purcell was born at exactly the right time. There is no need to wish that he could have lived later, when music was more 'settled'. Being a genius, he could thrive on the doubts and upheavals of the so-called 'transitional' period of the late seventeenth century. If he had been born sooner he would not only have missed the inestimable blessing of having Monteverdi and the Camerata behind him: he would also have been faced with the embarrassing riches of the Elizabethan poets. His tunes were not meant to be coupled lovingly to lines that were already brimful of their own verbal music. He needed verses that could be torn in shreds and tossed into the air. In his subtle and sensitive response to the possibilities of the English language he chose to be naïve and obvious whenever the tune demanded it. So he revelled in his 'imitations', writing the trill known as a 'shake' when the verses offered him the word 'shaking':

Ex. 114

From 'Sound the Trumpet'

His hands like shak — — — — — ing Li - lies play

and allowing the voice and trumpet to throw the word 'catch' to each other:

Ex. 115

The gesture, as always with Purcell, is perfectly timed, and the sung onomatopoeia is brilliantly matched by the trumpet's tongued attack.

Purcell found onomatopoeia irresistible. If the verses offered him the lines 'Hark, the ech'ing Air a triumph sings/And all around pleas'd Cupids clap their wings', he first silenced the listeners with the sudden gesture of a repeated 'Hark', and then swept the singer into a triumphant series of shakes and turns and fanfares and flourishes, finally encouraging his Cupids to clap and clap and go on clapping to the aptest of all rhythms:

Ex. 116

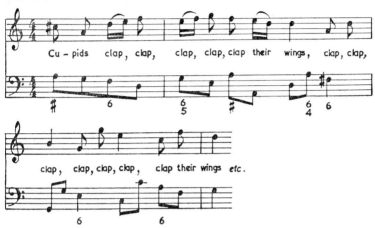

It is the chords in Ex. 116 which make it possible for the tune to be shaped with so many gapped intervals. Wide leaps were often a help to Purcell in creating his dramatic characters. When the Drunken Poet sings his six-eight tune in *The Fairy Queen* it takes him less than five bars to establish his musical personality:

Ex. 117

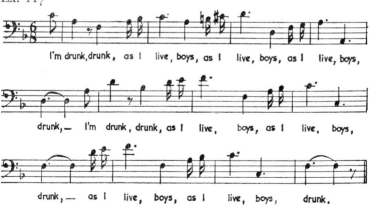

The libretto alone can tell us nothing about the Drunken Poet as a person. He might be just one of a multitude of nondescript, barely coherent unfortunates. But the tune brings him startlingly to life and makes him unique and unforgettable. He is gloriously happy, but not in the least noisy or undignified. He is slightly unsteady on his feet, but he can still keep upright; when he approaches his fellow actors as if he were about to embrace them on his top note, it is not because he is finding it difficult to remain on his feet—it is because he wants to impress them with the importance of what he is saying. The modulations help to underline the importance at each repetition, and the downward-sweeping octaves show that all his gestures are relaxed. The tune is so satisfying that it gives us confidence in him as a person: we are even ready to believe that he can write poetry when sober.

In Purcell's only real opera the hero has no aria: it is the melodic shape of his recitatives that brings Aeneas to life. Tate's libretto offers the mere shadow of a hero, but as soon as Purcell gets hold of him there is nothing shadowy about him. The one word 'Tonight?', sung on an indignant rising fifth, is enough to turn him into a human being. Dido has only just agreed to marry him, and now the gods are telling him that he must leave Carthage that very night. His sudden protest comes straight from the diaphragm, as if the quick tension of emotion had immediately sent his voice up to the next level of the harmonic series.

Tate's lines for Aeneas were just what Purcell needed, though when the words are read without any tune they strike an unpromising chill:

Dido. *Fate forbids what you Ensue.*

Aeneas. *Aeneas has no Fate but you.*
Let Dido smile and I'le defie
The Feeble stroke of Destiny.

The spoken verse limps, and the piling up of the repeated 'i' seems over-insistent. But Purcell lifts the words on the rising tide of Aeneas's emotion: the climax of 'defie' is like a drawn sword; the scorn of 'Feeble' sends the word withering downwards to its diminished fifth, while the emphatic rhythm of 'Destiny' is like a warning of the doom that is to come:

Ex. 118

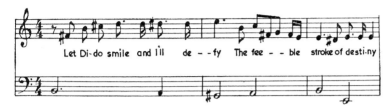

Let Di-do smile and I'll de--fy The fee--ble stroke of desti-ny

This is what Purcell's contemporaries meant by his 'genius for expressing the energy of the English language'. When a thunderstorm threatens, the energy of Belinda's 'Haste' sends her rushing on to the stage to interrupt Dido and Aeneas in their conversation:

Ex. 119

Haste, haste to town, haste, haste, haste, haste, haste _

_____ to town, haste, haste, haste, haste, *etc.*

The panting 'h' and the keen edge of the vowel combine to send her anxious voice up the 'natural' trumpet-notes of command. The tune is in keeping with Belinda's character; her kindly and competent warning to take shelter empties the stage of Queen and courtiers and huntsmen in less than two minutes.

When Tate's libretto reaches the perilous passages where the author begins explaining what is going to happen next, Purcell is never content to let his characters merely hand out information to the audience. 'Ruin'd ere the set of sun? Tell us, how shall this be done?' asks the leading Witch, supplying the Sorceress with a conventional cue for unfolding the plot. But Purcell's ear has seized the rhythm of that 'Tell us'; he brings in a second Witch to emphasize the question; they hammer at the words, 'tell us, tell us, tell us' until the audience is caught up and held by their lively curiosity:

Ex. 120

It is not only the rhythm of the repeated 'tell us' that gives the question its weight; it is also the pull of the harmony on the word 'how'. There was no need for Purcell to go through Peri's laborious process of deciding when the recitative needed a new bass to support it. The experimental stage was over, and the characters in *Dido and Aeneas* talked in harmony because it was their native language, with the rise and fall of their voices clearly expressing their feelings:

Ex. 121

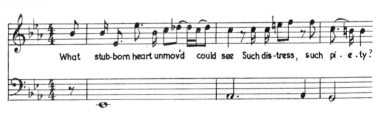

The melodic line of Ex. 121 has already moved beyond Dryden's definition of 'a kind of tuneful pronunciation': it is no less musical than song. Recitative such as this can slip easily in and out of the arias without destroying the continuity of each scene.

Dido's own songs are melodies rather than tunes: they need to be extended to convey the depth and magnitude of her tragedy. She can repeat her sentences over and over again, and sustain her long notes for bar after bar, without letting her songs lose the poignant directness of a simple tune. At the height of her dramatic intensity, the words 'Remember me' have the natural rhythm of a human appeal.

The simple tunes in *Dido and Aeneas* that are compact enough to be taken home and whistled are the short airs such as 'Fear no danger', where Purcell's unexpected accents destroy the spoken metre and create a lilting rhythm of their own:

Ex. 122

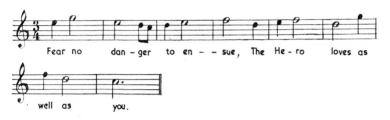

There is no need to grace this tune; it only needs what Caccini called a 'lively, cheerful kind of singing which is carried and ruled by the air itself'. It is one of those songs 'which being sung to a ditty may likewise be danced'.

CHAPTER VIII

Ayres for the Theatre

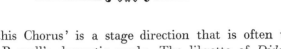

'Dance this Chorus' is a stage direction that is often to be found in Purcell's dramatic works. The libretto of *Dido and Aeneas* asks for 'Fear no danger' to be danced after it has been sung, and there are Song Tunes in *The Fairy Queen* and *King Arthur* where 'the Dance continues with the same Measure play'd alone'. Steps and figures replace the words, fitting their patterns to tunes that have already been shaped by the pattern of the verses.

There are Song Tunes in Purcell's posthumous *Ayres for the Theatre* for strings and continuo, but most of the tunes in the volume are Hornpipes and Minuets and Jiggs that have never needed the help of words to bring them to life:

Ex. 123

As a tune, it is just as compelling as any of Purcell's cheerful songs: his genius for expressing the energy of English words was equally at home in expressing the energy of English dances.

The Hornpipe from *The Virtuous Wife* triumphantly proves Busoni's assertion that a tune 'can exist independent of text for expression', and at the same time it shows how lamentably over-cautious he was in saying that a tune 'gives back a certain atmosphere of feeling'. Ex. 123 has far more to offer than a cheerful mood: its character is as clearly drawn and as unforgettable as the character of the Drunken Poet in Ex. 117.

The *Ayres for the Theatre,* like all Purcell's tunes, were written for a practical purpose. They were Act Tunes or Curtain Tunes to fill in the gaps during the changes of scene and to disguise the noise made in shifting those heavy machines that enabled messengers of the gods to sing in mid-air, supported by solid clouds.

Several of the Hornpipes became so popular that they were borrowed for Playford's *English Dancing Master* and were transformed into social ballroom dances. The tunes for Playford's country dances had to be as clear and compact as possible, for the amateur dancers could only remember their steps and figures if the tune itself reminded them of what to do next. In a dance where the figures were divided into several sections, each section of the tune had to have its own clearly defined shape and character:

Ex. 124

Mayden Lane

Playford

The dance figures were simple formulas strung together in a conventional order, with an introduction of 'lead up, forward and back', and a chorus of 'two steps to the right, two to the left, and a clockwise turn'. Many of the Playford tunes imitated these

formulas with the shape of their phrases; in the opening bars of
'The Merry Merry Milkmaids' (Ex. 125) the dancers would have
recognized that the tune was telling them exactly what to do:

Ex. 125

The Merry Merry Milkmaids

Playford

(*Then* | *lead your partner up,* and | *lead your partner back*; *and*
| *set to the right and set to the left, and* | *turn a single round.*)

Onlookers who sit and watch modern revivals of seventeenth-
century country dancing are often struck by the similarity between the sound and the movement: they notice the satisfying
patterns and are reminded of the suggestion that dancing is
music made visible. But the dancers, who are right inside the
music, think very differently about it. They are not concerned
with what their patterns look like from the outside: they only
know that the shape they are making with their steps and figures
feels the same as the shape of the tune, for movement is their
language. The '*long*-short, *long*-short' skipping step of a six-eight
Playford dance has the same feeling as the sung '*fa*-la, *la*-la'
of a Morley Canzonet, for the pressure of the tongue and its
flapping recoil shares the same effortless rhythm as the pressure
of the foot and its buoyant rebounding.

All this the dancer knows by feel, without having to think
about it. And he can enjoy the excitement of working out
mathematical patterns with human beings instead of with numbers. The return to his own partner at the end of a figure-of-eight
can have the expressive satisfaction of the return to the tonic at
the end of a tune.

Figures-of-eight and rings to the left or the right are formulas
that can be fitted to any tune that has a convincing shape and an
obvious rhythm and the right number of beats. That is perhaps
one of the reasons why Purcell's music has been described as the

easiest in the world to dance to. An *Ayre* such as Ex. 126, if fitted to a Playford dance of the same length, could straightway sound and feel as if it had always been intended for those steps and figures:

Ex. 126

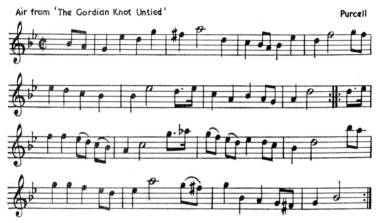

Air from 'The Gordian Knot Untied'   Purcell

In a song, this obvious time-pattern, with its same rising syncopation recurring at every alternate bar, might seem oversimple, but in a dance it is just what is needed.

It is not only in his energetic airs that Purcell uses such scanty material: in one of the most flowing of the Minuets he repeats the same simple time-pattern over and over again:

Ex. 127

Minuet from 'The Double Dealer'   Purcell

The dancer finds nothing frugal about this rhythm. The quavers are not steps, so there is no danger of his giving unnecessary emphasis to the repeated time-pattern. He moves to the harmony, being content, in the first half of the tune, with the simple to-and-fro of tonic and dominant. In the second half, the modulations encourage him to turn aside, before coming back to his partner for the final cadence.

The smoothly purposeful modulations in Purcell's *Ayres* make it easy, even at first hearing, to improvise dance movements to a tune such as Ex. 128, where the unfolding of the harmony seems to draw each gesture with it:

Ex. 128

When improvising a dance there is no need for the analytical mind to say to the body: 'Now move to the left; now bend down.' All that is needed is for the dancer to lean on the tune ungrudgingly, while keeping enough weight in reserve to carry him through to the end of the phrase, as a singer keeps his breath in reserve when sight-reading an aria. Listening then becomes something that concerns the whole person instead of just the ears. And this is the kind of listening that dance tunes are meant for. Audiences, sitting in rows, can share the dancer's excitement without knowing anything about steps or figures, for the feel of the dance is in the sound of the tune. And instrumentalists can give the dancer the phrasing that he wants without knowing how to move one foot after another, for if they follow the musical shape of the tune it will feel right to dance to.

CHAPTER IX

Bach's Tunes

Although the dances in Bach's Suites are not meant to be danced to, the tunes have inherited the rhythm and pattern of the sixteenth- and seventeenth-century Almans, Borres, Sarabands and Jiggs that they are founded on. They are sometimes described as 'idealized' dances, but this does not mean that they have lost their capacity for making the listener want to get up and dance. They are just as compelling as Purcell's *Ayres for the Theatre*, and the individual character of each tune is as clearly drawn as if it were to be danced on a stage:

Ex. 129

Bourrée I from Cello Suite in E♭

The line of this unaccompanied tune is so completely satisfying that it is able to carry on an imaginary conversation with itself: the rising semiquavers in bars 4–5 and 6–7 suggest the question and answer of polyphonic imitation. And, as always with Bach, the tune contains its own harmony. In many movements from the Suites for solo violin or cello the harmonies are played in a broken-chord texture, enabling the tune to carry its own accompaniment without burdening itself or losing its continuous melodic line:

Ex. 130

Courante from Cello Suite in C

These broken chords are another legacy from the sixteenth and seventeenth centuries: they are the conventional formulas for the 'divisions' which were handed on from one composer to another. The musical language was common property, and any learner could take what he wanted from such textbooks as Christopher Simpson's *The Division Viol*, finding hundreds of examples of 'Breaking or Dividing a Note into more diminutive Notes'. The small notes could be 'imployed in making a Transition':

Ex. 131[1]

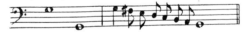

Or they could be 'imployed in skipping into other Concords':

Ex. 132

---

[1] Examples 131–133b are taken from Christopher Simpson, *The Division Viol*, facsimile edition, Curwen, 1955.

And the notes of an ostinato bass such as Ex. 133 could be divided in the simplest of the dialogue styles that Purcell so often borrowed for a Ground (Ex. 133a) or in the more elaborately graced style of Ex. 133b which sounds as if it might be the beginning of a movement by Bach:

Ex. 133

Ex. 133a

Ex. 133b

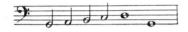

In Bach's hands, these well-worn scale passages and broken chords spring to life and become tunes:

Ex. 134

Prelude from the Cello Suite in C

Even in this opening bar, the shape of the conventional division has a character that is unforgettable.

There are Preludes that consist of nothing but a series of broken chords, yet the music never loses its individuality:

Ex. 135

Prelude from Cello Suite in G

The melodic line in Ex. 135 is not a restless pattern of sixteen semiquavers to the bar: it is a calm journey of one harmony moving on to the next.

The underlying harmonies of these broken-chord Preludes are easiest to explore in the keyboard works; the groups of semiquavers in Ex. 136 can be gathered together to form the chords that they have grown out of (Ex. 136a):

Ex. 136

Praeludium

Ex. 136a

The most elaborately graced of the slow dance movements can be explored in the same way. On paper, the keyboard Allemande in Ex. 137 looks complicated, with its written-out ornaments and its waywardly contrapuntal texture, but its underlying chords in Ex. 137a move from one harmony to the next as easily as in the simplest dance:

Ex. 137

Allemande from the French Suite No. 2

Ex. 137a

A dancer, listening for the first time to the Allemande in Ex. 137, could improvise steps and figures to it by moving to the harmonies. There would be no need for him to worry about the exact time-patterns of the ornaments, for he could rely on his gestures coinciding with the outline of the melody. And in the same way, a listener who could feel the movement of the harmony would be able to carry away with him a sense of the melodic shape, even though he might have forgotten most of the details of the embroidery.

Ex. 137 is a melody rather than a tune, for it is not compact

116

enough to be taken home and whistled after one hearing. The famous Air from the Overture in D is also a melody, for it extends beyond the proportions of a simple tune. It is neither too long nor too elaborate to be held in the memory, and there must be hundreds of music-lovers who have never tried to play it but who have heard it so many times that they could whistle it through from beginning to end without forgetting any detail; but the melody, when whistled, is not self-supporting. The long-sustained notes need their accompaniment to keep them alive, just as Dowland's 'Arise' in 'Sorrow, stay' (Ex. 104, p. 90) needs the moving accompaniment of the lute to store up new energy while the voice remains effortlessly floating at the same level of sound.

The compact tunes in Bach's music are the chorales. Some are his own original tunes, but most are borrowed from the traditional songs that Luther transformed into congregational hymns. These transformations are as startling as anything that has ever happened in music: the German folk song in Ex. 138 manages to shed all its previous associations and turn itself into a hymn with an entirely different mood and tempo and expression and meaning (Ex. 138a):

Ex. 138[1]

[1] *Altdeutsches Liederbuch*, ed. F. M. Böhme, Breitkopf & Härtel, 1913.

Ex. 138a

The transformation from plainsong to chorale is just as astonishing. The freely flowing rhythm of *Veni Creator Spiritus* (Ex. 139) is relentlessly clamped down to provide firm beats for the organ chorale in Ex. 139a:

Ex. 139

Ex. 139a

The tune of *Komm, Gott Schöpfer* is a distortion, but the result is worth it. The four-square framework of the chorale has become as strong a foundation as the tune in Ex. 140:

Ex. 140

From 'Wachet auf' Cantata No. 140

Here the tune's deliberate steps, marking out the length and direction of each line, are able to build such an unshakable fabric that no listener could ever be in danger of getting lost. He could hear the arrival of the traditional tune in Ex. 140 out of the corner of one ear, while listening to the warmth of Bach's own obligato tune.

Without the help of the chorales, the members of the congregation of St. Thomas's Church in Leipzig might well have complained that Bach's music was too difficult for them to understand. But Bach never forgot them. Every Sunday he gave them the tunes they wanted, not just as a couple of congregational hymns and an organ voluntary, but as the central statement of his cantatas. Knowing the hymns by heart, the ordinary listeners in the congregation were able to follow a chorale tune throughout the longest chorus, waiting, during the elaborate instrumental interludes, for the entry of the next familiar line from the sopranos and trumpets, or recognizing the clear notes of the *cantus firmus* in the interweaving of the vocal counterpoint.

Bach's listeners could even keep a tenuous hold of the tune throughout its variations; having sung the chorale *Jesu meine Freude* (Ex. 141) they could recognize its influence in the shatteringly unexpected version of Ex. 141a:

Ex. 141

Je-su mei-ne Freu - - de,

Ex. 141a

Trotz, Trotz dem al - - ten Dra - - chen

The sudden defiance in this opening phrase is in the direct
tradition of Monteverdi: the isolated word 'Trotz' stands out like
an abrupt gesture on an operatic stage. Although the word merely
means 'in spite of', it has managed to keep the onomatopoeic
venom of the kind of spite that is contemptuous. The fierce consonants, having launched the sound with a spurt of energy,
immediately cut it short, so that the opening discord is made even
more dramatic by hitting against a shocked silence.

Consonants often help in the shaping of Bach's tunes. The
'schweigt, schweigt' of Ex. 142 brings with its spoken sound a
well-marked staccato that demands the energy of gapped intervals. (The alto's gesture of impatience breaks into the question,
'When shall we see Him?')

Ex. 142

From the Christmas Oratorio

The usual translation for Ex. 142 is 'Peace, peace, peace, for
surely this is He.' But alas, the sense of urgency evaporates, and
the tune loses its musical meaning. 'Hush, hush' would be better,
but it is still too mild to match the clear-cut staccato.

Inadequate translations drain the energy from Bach's tunes
and destroy their wonderful balance of tension and relaxation.
In the sentence 'Ihr aber seid nicht fleischlich, sondern geistlich',
the comma comes between the seventh and eighth syllables, and
Bach sets the phrase accordingly:

Ex. 143

From 'Jesu meine Freude'

Bach has shaped his tune so as to allow for a moment of relaxation at the comma, before an energetic new attack on 'sondern'. In the English translation, 'Ye are not of the flesh, but of the spirit', the comma comes a syllable too soon, wrecking the resolution of the suspension on 'fleischlich', ironing out the buoyancy of the leaping fourth and arriving with an unavoidable accent on the word 'of'. Yet nothing is done to repair the damage, since the words are a direct quotation from St. Paul.

If only we could rid ourselves of an over-reverent approach in translating passages from the Bible we might avoid losing so much of the drama in Bach's Passion music. When the hostile crowd in the *St. John Passion* thrusts its way up to Pilate saying 'Wir haben ein Gesetz', the mood of the argument is clearly stated in the tune:

Ex. 144

Wir ha-ben ein Ge – setz   und nach dem Ge - setz soll er ster-(ben)

The quavers are clipped with a malignant deliberation that makes the listener shudder. But in the translation these quavers are linked together to fit the words 'We have a law': the expressive slurs smooth away all bitterness and reduce the living characters in the drama to a sawdust incompetence. Two more syllables are needed to save the tune: 'We have an ancient law' helps the rhythm, but nothing can replace the churlishness of that final 'tz'.

When the crowd shouts 'Kreuzige!' the tune owes its energy to the structure of the spoken syllables:

Ex. 145

Kreu - zi - ge,   kreu - zi - ge,

The English word 'crucify' is unable to stand up to the energy of this time-pattern. The soft hiss of the 'ci' is not strong enough to articulate the first semiquaver: the note needs the resistance of the 'tz'. And the wide open English 'y' allows no chance of a rapid relaxation before the new attack. The repetition, which is rhythmically balanced in German, becomes uncontrollable in English, and as a result the tune is in danger of disintegrating into dotted triplets. I have found during rehearsals that it is better to mispronounce the English word, turning it into 'Kroo-tziffe(r)', rather than risk losing the rhythm of Bach's tune. And in the second part of the same chorus, the words 'Away with him, away' need to be sung 'Way, way with him, way, way' in order to get enough weight for attacking the quavers (Ex. 146):

Ex. 146

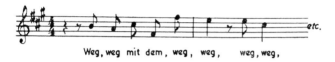

Weg, weg mit dem, weg, weg, weg, weg,

When the orchestral strings join in with vigorous quavers at each 'weg, weg', the roughness of the pressure on the bow matches the violence of the sung 'v'. And at the end of each stroke, when the bow abruptly flicks the note away, the sudden break in the sound matches the 'ck' of the voices. Because of this wordless onomatopoeia, the frequent doubling of the instrumental and vocal lines in Bach's choruses adds to the clarity of the settings. The doubling was an inevitable result of economic necessity: he had only five sopranos, two altos, three tenors and seven basses in his choir for the usual Sunday cantatas.[1] But his music flourished on having to make both ends meet. He told his players to phrase according to the sense of the words,[2] and this advice remains the best guide through the thickets of twentieth-century musicological arguments about style and tempo.

In the *St. John Passion*, the style of the string playing at 'Hail, King of the Jews' manages to avoid the unwanted cheerfulness of a dance tune by stressing the gritty, grating sound of the singers' 'Sei gegrüsset':

[1] C. S. Terry, *Bach's Orchestra*, Oxford University Press, London, 1932, p. 9.
[2] *The Bach Reader*, ed. H. T. David and A. Mendel, Norton, New York, 1945, p. 237.

Ex. 147

The mood of this mock dance is so overwhelmingly cruel that there is scarcely any need for the Evangelist to tell us that 'they smote him with their hands'. It is hardly surprising that the old lady who sat in the front pew at the first performance protested that she might just as well have been at the opera.[1]

But it is not only in the Passions that Bach's tunes follow the mood and gesture of the words with an energy that is operatic. In the *B Minor Mass* the familiar words of the Gloria and the Credo sound as exciting as if they were being sung for the first time. The simple tune at 'Et in terra pax' is subtly shaped by the meaning that the words had in Bach's mind: the smoothly flowing quavers are as peaceful as any bar of music that has yet been written; mankind steps purposefully along its straightforward syllabic path, and the sum of all the goodwill in the world sends the voice skipping up a seventh, with a carefree turn at the top of the tune:

Ex. 148

This turn at 'bonae voluntatis' is borrowed from one of the hundred-year-old formulas for an instrumental division (see Ex. 133b), but the placing is so right that the sentence comes as a revelation.

Bach, like Purcell, was never afraid of sounding obvious. The words 'came down from heaven' inevitably draw the strings downwards through two octaves of a dominant seventh arpeggio. And at 'ascended into heaven' the chorus basses are lifted bodily

[1] See *The Bach Reader*, p. 229.

from their lowest notes to the very highest rim of their compass;
they hover for an instant at the new level of the modulation,
and then seat themselves with a relaxed sense of arrival:

Ex. 149

as – cen – – dit in coe-lum, se-det

Gapped intervals, with their balanced tension and relaxation,
conjure up an astonishingly confident semblance of the Father
Almighty:

Ex. 150

Pa-trem o-mni-po-ten – tem,facto-rum coe – li et ter - - rae

The falling major seventh, which in other contexts in Bach's
music can sound so strained and tragic, is here benign in its
relaxation. There is enjoyment in the creation of heaven and
earth—an enjoyment that is like Bach's own unparalleled delight
in building melodies on a foundation of harmony.

This obvious enjoyment can tell us more about Bach as a
person than any biographical details. There is no need to bewail
the fact that very few of his letters survive, or that they are only
concerned with testimonials and receipts and complaints to the
Leipzig authorities about the need for practical improvements in
his working conditions. We know about his own character as soon
as we hear the characteristic tunes that he gives to each of the
Persons of the Trinity in the *B Minor Mass*: the vitality of the
'Patrem omnipotentem' is inseparable from the tenderness of the
'Domine Deus' (Ex. 151), which is surely one of the loveliest
formulas ever 'imployed in making a Transition':

Ex. 151

(Flute)

And the vitality and the tenderness are both contained in the dancing radiance of the tune for the Holy Spirit:

Ex. 152

The 'Cum Sancto Spiritu' was built for close canonic imitation, with voices entering only a crotchet apart. Yet the tune never feels restricted: it moves as freely as if it were concerned with nothing but its own horizontal line. Bach thought so fugally that he was always aware of everything that could happen to a tune. Carl Philip Emmanuel has described how his father used to listen to an organist improvising a fugue: 'He could soon say, after the first entries of the subjects, what contrapuntal devices it would be possible to apply . . . and on such occasions, when I was standing next to him and he had voiced his surmises to me, he would joyfully nudge me when his expectations were fulfilled.'[1]

Being so much at home in the language of fugue, he could write subjects that sound as simple as a folk song:

Ex. 153

But in the working out of this fugue the harmonic counterpoint is closely packed and intricate:

Ex. 153a

---

[1] Ibid., p. 277.

etc.

Here the original tune is barely recognizable. But it has not lost its identity: it has gained in expression as a result of meeting the challenge of such independent part-writing.

No composer has ever got more out of a tune than Bach. Byrd and his friend Alphonso Ferrabosco could spend their free time in tossing off forty different polyphonic settings of the same *cantus firmus*, but no one has ever done what Bach did to the four-bar tune in *The Art of Fugue*. And because of this stupendous skill he has been labelled "the musicians' composer", a title as forbidding as the school-book description of Spenser as "the poets' poet". It is true that Bach is the musicians' composer in the sense that there can never be an end to discovering the riches in his music. But he is also the amateurs' composer, for his tunes make such sense in themselves that they can withstand the lapses of the learner, and only shrivel up in the hands of the insensitive. And he is certainly the listeners' composer, for he never forgot that the members of his Leipzig congregation needed tunes that they could live with.

CHAPTER X

Late Eighteenth-century
Themes and Subjects

To turn from Bach's tunes to those of his son Carl Philip Emmanuel is like going from one country to another, or from one century to the next:

Ex. 154

One of the most obvious changes of style is in the tempo indication. None of J. S. Bach's tunes could have survived being taken *presto di molto*. The new quick tunes, with their rapidly beating pulse, had to keep to the simplest of harmonies to avoid sounding hysterical. And they had to abstain from too much counterpoint to avoid sounding muddled.

In order to colour the plain chords and enliven the homo-phonic texture, composers allowed their tunes a plentiful supply of dynamics. Sudden changes from forte to piano, which Schütz and Purcell had used on special occasions, now became essential to the ordinary progress of a tune. Sudden silences were no longer kept for moments of drama: they were used as a normal method of punctuating journeys between the tonic and the dominant:

Ex. 155

As a tune, Ex. 155 is disappointing, though mid-eighteenth-century performers may have found it exciting enough to be able to rush at a furious speed from one level to another of the tonic chord. If Wagenseil's twelve-bar journey sounds perfunctory to our ears, it is not because there is anything inadequate in his harmonic formula, it is because he had not sufficient genius to sustain a flow of memorable tonic-to-dominant tunes.

From the very beginning, Haydn's tunes were unforgettable:

Ex. 156

This is as characteristic of Haydn as any of the tunes in his more mature works. But it is not characteristic of a first-movement subject. At the time when he wrote it, Haydn was still exploring the possibilities of form in his string quartets. He soon found that a cheerful six-eight horn-call such as Ex. 156 was likely to feel more at home in a last-movement rondo, where it could keep its original shape intact.

His after-dinner audiences—those hunting and shooting friends of the Esterházys—must have found the rondo tunes, with their identical repetitions, the easiest of all to take home and whistle. The slow-movement themes could also be held in the memory, for although the variations were elaborately graced, with frequent changes of texture and mood, the airs were nearly always as simple and straightforward as a song. And the quick Minuet tunes were as easy to listen to as their slower seventeenth-century predecessors had been to dance to.

It was in his first movements that Haydn's tunes needed a special kind of listening. In the Esterházy performances, the amateur musicians in the audience were perhaps the only listeners who were able to recognize what was happening to the tune in Ex. 157 during its development:

Ex. 157

The opening subject of a first movement had to be built in such a way that it could bear to have fragments torn out of it. The lively continuity of this theme shows no sign that it is about to be broken up into small pieces. But fragments are separated from it, and pulled inside out and turned upside down. At a moment of suspense, the rising sweep of the slurred crotchets is isolated and transformed into a dramatic downward curve:

Ex. 157a

And a gentler downward curve is heard in the *dolce* second subject of Ex. 157b—a tune that has borrowed its quavers from the fourth bar of Ex. 157:

Ex. 157b

This drastic treatment, far from killing the original tune, has given it an extended life, for the fragmentary cells produce new tunes of their own. And the fragments are sturdy enough to endure the stretching and buffeting of a development section. It is here that the drama in the music comes nearest to the classical development of a drama in words, with the process of complication, crisis and solution. But listeners who are following the adventures of a tune must not expect to be given a map or plan of action to guide them. No development section is like any other:

the drama unfolds according to the character of the tune. And there is no telling what Haydn may choose to do at any moment. Who could possibly guess, at a first hearing of Op. 54 no. 2, that the first violin's tune in Ex. 157 is immediately going to begin all over again in the remote key of A flat?

Yet in spite of the enthralling unexpectedness of Haydn and Mozart, the textbooks still try to tell their readers what to 'look out for' in first-movement sonata form. It is as unsatisfactory as being told to look out for a particular view during a train journey; while the traveller presses his nose to the window, mile after mile of eventful countryside flashes past unnoticed. Written analysis has only a clinical interest, and the fragment in Ex. 157a has very little meaning until it has become part of the remembered sound of the whole movement.

The only satisfying way to find out what happens to a tune in a development section is to get to know the sound of the music so thoroughly that the separate fragments link themselves together in a continuous texture, as in the piling up of the entries of a *cantus firmus* in sixteenth-century polyphony. And when each movement of a quartet or symphony or sonata has become familiar, the listening ear recognizes fragments of tunes that link one movement to the next. It is only then that the form of the whole work becomes clear.

Tunes in late eighteenth-century music are like well organized characters in a novel. One of the best descriptions of what happens to tunes in sonata form is the chapter called 'Pattern and Rhythm' in E. M. Forster's *Aspects of the Novel*. He has been talking about the suitability of the pattern of a book to the author's mood, and he says 'at the end we discover to our delight that [the characters] . . . have done the exact thing which the book requires, which it required from the start, and have bound the scattered incidents together with a thread woven out of their own substance'.

The ordinary listener who hears a Haydn or Mozart quartet for the first time cannot hope to hear everything. But he can get a great deal from the performance, for a good quartet, like a good poem, can 'communicate before it is understood'. Mozart himself said of one of his works: 'There are passages here and there from which connoisseurs alone can derive satisfaction; but these passages are written in such a way that the less learned cannot fail to be pleased, though without knowing why.'[1]

The less learned listeners are continually helped by the simplicity of Mozart's tunes. When he begins his D major quartet (K.499) with the bare octaves of Ex. 158, the tune sounds as easy and inevitable as any of the Mari folk songs in Chapter II:

Ex. 158

There are tunes built on a tonic-dominant formula on each of the nine hundred pages of Köchel's thematic catalogue of Mozart's works, yet every tune has its own individuality. The instrumental phrases sing their meaning as clearly as if they had been shaped by the words of a song:

Ex. 159

The language of the conversation in Ex. 159 is deliberately formal. But it is the courteous formality of normal eighteenth-century phrasing and gesture: heads had to be held upright, owing to the weight of the wig; movements had to be controlled to avoid collisions with the wide-swinging, stiffly wired hoops of the skirts; sentences had to be balanced and words chosen with precision if they were to be acceptable.

Mozart was incapable of writing an ill-balanced musical sen-

[1] *The Letters of Mozart and his Family*, trans. Emily Anderson, Macmillan, London, 1938 (letter of 28 December 1782).

tence. 'Passions', he explained to his father, 'must never be expressed in such a way as to excite disgust, and . . . music, even in the most terrible situations, must never offend the ear, but must please the hearer, or in other words must never cease to be music.'[1]

In his passionate tunes the intense emotions are hidden beneath the poised surface of the music:

Ex. 160

The falling semitone is as expressive in Mozart's bare octaves as in the four-part chromatic harmonies of a Bach chorale. And at the end of the movement, when the music grows too passionate for the rising octave and the tune has to leap with the rare tension of a minor ninth, the ear is not offended, for the violence in the interval has already been hinted at in the expressive falling semitone. The thread of sound that heightens the emotion has been woven out of the tune's own substance.

The most expressive moment in the passionate G minor string quintet is the arrival of the deceptively simple major tune in the finale:

Ex. 161

Heard away from its context, the tune has the direct charm and appeal of an Austrian folk song. But when it is heard where it

[1] Ibid. (26 September 1781).

belongs, the word 'charm' is no longer appropriate. The tune, for all its childlike simplicity, is a summing up of everything that has gone before: it is an answer to the agonizing question in those long-drawn-out crescendos of the second Adagio.

It is the extraordinary balance in his music that enables Mozart to put light-hearted tunes next to tragic tunes in *The Magic Flute*. The same warmth and seriousness flows through every note of every tune, whatever the mood of the moment may be. When Papageno's lips are closed with a padlock, the tune he hums has the poised clarity of an instrumental entry in a quartet, yet it is shaped by the bouncing energy of his indignant protest:

Ex. 162

'I like an aria to fit a singer as perfectly as a well-made suit of clothes,' Mozart once wrote after a rehearsal.[1] Schikaneder must have enjoyed singing Ex. 162: his delight is as audible as Papageno's discomfort. The four bars are a brilliant piece of characterization: we can hear what the unfortunate bird-catcher wants to say as clearly as if the words had not been locked up behind his lips. And the gesture of his indignation can be recognized in the insistence of the repeated notes and the blustering rise and fall of the accented intervals.

The gesture of the 'farewell' in Ex. 163 is as direct and obvious as if it were meant to be danced in a ballet:

Ex. 163

---

[1] Ibid. (28 February 1778).

It is the conversational word that has shaped the expressive outline of Ex. 163, but its cadence is borrowed from an instrumental formula. With Mozart, as with Bach, there is no rigid dividing line between instrumental melodies and sung arias. In the quartets, the instruments sing or act as if they were on the stage, and in the operas the characters express themselves with the organized forethought of subjects in a sonata.

The melody of Pamina's great aria in *The Magic Flute* could just as well have been an instrumental slow movement:

Ex. 164

Only Mozart could have written this, with its expressive change from minor to major at the word 'fühl', and its calm rise to a high B flat that leaves the balance of tension and relaxation undisturbed. Yet the ingredients of the music are all borrowed from a familiar traditional language: the poignancy of the diminished fifth at 'ewig' has been heard over and over again in the music of Bach and Purcell and Monteverdi, and the exquisite sound of the falling F natural against the rising F sharp is a legacy from the sixteenth-century polyphonists. And beneath the graces of its ornamental covering there is the outline of a tune that is as simple as a folk song. Because of its simplicity, the tragic aria sounds thoroughly at home with such popular tunes as Papageno's Glockenspiel dance. The whole opera is a mixture, but the different worlds overlap until they merge into each other.

This is perhaps what the textbooks mean when they talk about the 'classical perfection' of Mozart's music and the balance of thought and feeling in his works. Mozart himself spoke of 'the golden mean', and in a moment of depression he wrote to his father saying 'The golden mean of truth in all things is no longer either known or appreciated. In order to win applause one must write stuff which is so inane that a *fiacre* could sing it, or so unintelligible that it pleases precisely because no sensible man can understand it.'[1]

In his own music he was content with 'a happy medium between what is too easy and too difficult'.

[1] Ibid. (28 December 1782).

137

CHAPTER XI

Nineteenth-century Melodies

It was in November 1821 that Schubert's *Original Dances* (Op. 9) were published. Three months later, the Vienna Carnival borrowed them in a pirated version for the guitar, which was becoming a popular instrument for light music. The Carnival organizers liked to provide their patrons with a musical novelty each year, and Schubert's waltzes were just what they needed. For the tunes made an immediate appeal, and they could be whistled straight away:

Ex. 165

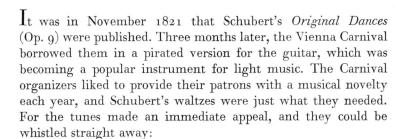

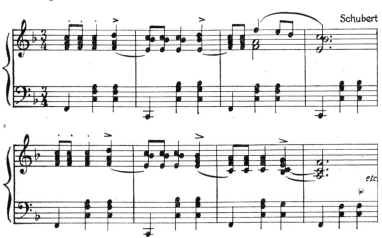

It is still the familiar tonic-dominant formula of the late eighteenth century, but in a very different dress. There was no longer any need for heads to be held upright, now the weight of the high-piled wigs had been removed. Ringlets hanging like petals of a flower allowed their wearers to indulge in a becoming droop of the head, first over one shoulder and then over the other. Skirts still billowed out, but waists were accessible now that the stiff wire cages had gone. With the new freedom of movement, a new lilt came into the to-and-fro of the harmonies. The one-in-a-bar rhythm encouraged frequent crescendos and diminuendos within the longer rise and fall of each eight-bar phrase. Tunes such as Ex. 166 could support the increasing tension of wider and wider intervals in the legato outline, without losing the ease of their simple harmonic structure:

Ex. 166

The newly invented waltzes were far more graceful than the heavier-footed Austrian Ländler that had given them birth. But the influence of the traditional folk dance could still be heard in tunes such as Ex. 167:

Ex. 167

The drawing-room charm of Ex. 167 is not so far removed from the open-air vitality of the traditional 'Juchzer' in Ex. 168:

Ex. 168[1]

Tyrolean Folk Song

Hol-di rai-de-rai — dai, di-rai ri-di-rai ho, hol-de- -ri di-rai-di-o, hol-de-ri di-rai-di-o! Hol-di -rai-de-rai-dai di rai ri-di-rei-ho, hol-de- -rai di-rai-di-o, hol-da-ro!

This close link with nineteenth-century folk song is something that we in England find difficult to understand. We are used to thinking of folk songs as ancient tunes that have had to be revived, and it is not easy to image them as popular and contemporary. Schubert, in his waltzes, managed to combine the best of all worlds; the tunes were new and yet rooted in tradition, city bred though at home in the mountains, and highly successful as a background to conversation in the cafés, but at the same time imperishable. The Viennese of the 1820's who whistled them on their way to work were luckier than they could realize. Many of the tunes have been lost to us, for Schubert improvised them during some of the evenings he spent with his friends. We are

[1] *Echte Tiroler Volkslieder*, Verlagsanstalt Tyrolia, Innsbruck.

given tantalizing glimpses of these meetings in the letters written from one friend to another: 'Last night we were at your mother's with Schubert. . . . A meal, and afterwards a little dance.'[1]

The published tunes often sound like improvisations:

Ex. 169

[1] O. E. Deutsch, *Schubert; A Documentary Biography*, Dent, London, 1946, p. 299.

Schubert's waltzes sound as if an endless stream of other tunes were still lying waiting, stored up within the harmonic framework, just as folk songs are stored up within the framework of a mode. They are always satisfying to dance to, for their rhythm is tirelessly balanced. The modulating tunes no longer suggest the intricate twists and turns of the patterned dances of the seventeenth century; here the augmented sixths and enharmonic changes lift the dancers into a floating rubato at the approach to each cadence.

It is the same warmth that flows through the melodies in Schubert's symphonies and chamber music:

Ex. 170

In his *Music in the Romantic Era*[1] Alfred Einstein says that 'with Schubert, beautiful melody is an end in itself', whereas 'the quality of the melody, as such, had little significance for Beethoven'. In discussing Schubert's piano works he says that the themes 'have their felicity in themselves and . . . resist dissection [or] development'. But this does not mean that Schubert's inexhaustible flow of beautiful tunes prevented him from gathering his music together with a thread woven from its own substance. When he was only nineteen he already knew what it was in Mozart's G minor quintet that brought the light out of the darkness. And in his own C major quintet the mood and structure of the whole work can be heard in the opening bars of the first movement. The beautiful melodies in the quintet remain in the memory, as beautiful melodies always will remain. But they are not self-sufficient tunes: they are the essential melodic lines on which the form of the work depends. And the overwhelming impression after hearing a performance is of the wholeness of the music.

It was this sense of wholeness that enabled Schubert to write

[1] A. Einstein, *Music in the Romantic Era*, Norton, New York, pp. 91, 55, 95.

his song cycles. In *Die schöne Müllerin,* the brook's rippling accompaniment changes in speed and pattern and texture with the changing mood of each poem, being caught up into the sound of the huntsman's horn during the impetuous jealousy of 'Die böse Farbe' and becoming reconciled with that sound during the calm acceptance of the final 'Wiegenlied'.

The singer's tunes in *Die schöne Müllerin* never lose the direct simplicity of their words:

Ex. 171

The gesture is as obvious as the 'Auf Wiedersehen' in *The Magic Flute,* and it is equally memorable. But the twenty tunes in *Die schöne Müllerin* cannot be taken home and sung in solitude as if they were a collection of twenty folk songs, for the tunes are only half alive without the partnership of their accompaniment. It is impossible to think of the dotted rhythm of 'Ungeduld' (Ex. 172) without remembering the sound of the piano's impatient triplets:

Ex. 172

grüb es gern in je — den Kie — sel-stein,

The partnership is as close as when Dowland played his own accompaniments while singing his lutenist songs. Schubert himself has described the inseparable link between singer and pianist. In a letter of 1825 he says: 'The manner in which Vogl sings and the way I accompany, as though we were one at such a moment, is something quite new and unheard-of for these people.'[1]

It was also something quite new for listeners to hear the pianist setting the scene for each new song with such a wealth of imagination and with so few notes. The brief introduction to 'Der Neugierige' (Ex. 173) subtly conveys the mood of questioning with its two wisps of sound and the balanced silence that lies between them:

Ex. 173

Die Neugierige

Langsam

Sixty-five years later, Hugo Wolf was borrowing this same economical device for setting the stage in his Lieder. The melancholy falling diminished fifths in the introduction to 'Das verlassene Mägdlein' (Ex. 174) say all that has to be said with a harmonic restraint that is already feeling its way towards the twentieth century; the pianist's influence is so all-pervading that

[1] Deutsch, op. cit., p. 458.

the singer's perfect fifths lose their assurance and become tinged with the same unhappiness:

Ex. 174

Das verlassene Mägdlein   Wolf

Früh, wann die Häh - ne krähn, eh' die Stern-lein schwin - den,

Schubert's immediate successors were more inclined to be carried away by the exciting possibilities of the nineteenth-century piano. In Schumann's *Dichterliebe* the piano's long melodic postludes often have more to say than the voice.

Tunes on the piano tend to become melodies carrying their own accompaniments with them. It is perilous to try to echo a singer's slowly sung phrase in naked notes on the keyboard, for the player's expressive intervals start dying away just when they should be growing in warmth and intensity. A flowing accompaniment is an obvious help in covering up the deficiency, and the listening ear can be cheated into believing that the long notes in the melody are as sustained as if they were being sung. It is only when the slow rise or fall of a melodic phrase is in need of a diminuendo that it can safely be entrusted to the single notes or bare octaves of the piano. But even then there is the problem of intonation. Equal-tempered melodic triads, if played slowly, need to be veiled in a contrapuntal texture or covered up with chords: when they are left naked they can sound embarrassingly out of tune. The piano's bare octaves in the fifth and sixth bars of Mozart's piano quartet in E flat often come as a shock. They must have been easier to manage with the dry attack of the eighteenth-century fortepiano, but with the sonorous mellow cantabile of the modern piano they need meticulous care in balance and phrasing if they are to sound in tune with the strings.

The great pianist-composers of the nineteenth century knew all that was to be known about disguising the shortcomings of their favourite instrument. When Schumann wrote tunes for children to play on the piano he was seldom content with 'melody for the right hand and harmony for the left'. In 'Erinnerung' (Ex. 175) the hands contrive to allow the melody to merge into its harmonies:

Ex. 175

Erinnerung — Schumann Op. 68

Nicht schnell und sehr gesangvoll zu spielen

The intermittent counterpoint in Ex. 175 reveals the inadequacy of the too easy nineteenth-century definition of melody as 'the upper outline of a series of different chords'. But although the definition is clumsy, there is some truth in it. For chords need not be solid, and outlines can draw their way through passing notes and appoggiaturas. The tune in Ex. 175 belongs to its harmonies in very much the same way that Bach's tunes grow from their figured basses.

In Schumann's 'Bittendes Kind' (Ex. 176) the 'upper outline' loses its meaning when separated from its chords. Heard in isolation, the melodic intervals spell out different harmonies from those in Schumann's mind, just as the pentatonic tunes in Chapter II could spell out the wrong harmonies unless they were heard in relation to their own mode:

Ex. 176

The melodies in *Kinderscenen* are among the most memorable that Schumann ever wrote. There is a revealing sentence in the letter in which he describes them to Clara: 'I suddenly got an inspiration and knocked off about thirty quaint little things, from which I have selected twelve, and called them "Kinderscenen". They will amuse you, but of course you must forget you are a performer.'[1] It is this last sentence that is so revealing. Mozart would never have had to say that to his sister Nannerl when he sent her a new set of piano pieces. But in the nineteenth century, simplicity was romantic. As Schumann explained in another letter to Clara: 'The romantic element does not depend upon figures and forms; it will always appear if the composer is anything of a poet. I would make all this much clearer to you on the piano, with a few "Kinderscenen".'[2]

It is always easier to make it clear at the piano. In conversation, the word 'romantic' too often muddles the mind. Writers can describe Schubert as 'a romantic classic', or they may prefer to call him 'a classical romantic', but neither description gets us any further. It is only 'at the piano', or from right inside his music, that the words begin to have any meaning.

It is perhaps less dangerous to distinguish between the true romantic and the romantic Romantic, for the true romantic always cares passionately about making things clear. Schumann himself, when he was still a student, wrote to a young friend, saying: 'Feelings are stars which can only guide you in a clear sky.'[3] And Blake spoke for the true romantic when he said: 'A Spirit and a Vision are not, as the modern philosophy supposes, a cloudy vapour or a nothing; they are organized and minutely articulated beyond all that the mortal and perishing nature can produce.'

It was his passionate concern for clarity that made Verdi protest against Wagner's music. He insisted that art which was lacking in naturalness and simplicity could not be called art. His own tunes were minutely articulated in the directness of their expression:

[1] *Schumann's Early Letters*, p. 264.
[2] Ibid., p. 287.
[3] Ibid., p. 3.

Ex. 177

From the Requiem — Verdi

Largo con molto espressione
♩=60

La-cry - mo - sa di - es__ il - la, Qua re - - - sur-get ex fa -

-vil - la, Ju - di - can-dus ho - mo re - us, Hu - ic er-go parce De - - us.

The style is nineteenth-century, with its rising sequences and its frequent crescendos and diminuendos, but the shape is as balanced as the classically perfect tunes of Mozart. In aiming at naturalness in his tunes, Verdi borrowed whatever well-worn formulas he needed, for he was unmoved by the romantic Romantics' struggle for originality at all costs.

In Germany the struggle could be very exhausting at times, and Schumann had to drop a hint to his Leipzig students that 'an occasional reminiscence' was 'preferable to a desperate independence'.[1] There were other composers, however, who would not have agreed with him. Wagner was furious when a critic pointed out that he had been borrowing. In a letter to von Bülow he complained of the indiscretion, saying: 'Since my acquaintance with Liszt's compositions I have become a quite different person —so far as my harmonic style is concerned. But when Pohl goes blabbing to all the world this secret at the very beginning of a discussion of the Prelude to *Tristan* . . .'[2]

To feel ashamed of borrowing was a romantic weakness that broke away from the musical tradition of at least nineteen hundred years. Another break with tradition was caused by the romantic disinclination for writing commissioned works. 'With Beethoven', says Einstein,[3] 'there began a period in which symphonies, oratorios, lyric and choral [and] chamber music of every kind, and even operas were written without being ordered, for an imaginary public, for the future, and if possible for "eternity."

[1] Schumann, *On Music and Musicians*, p. 80.
[2] Einstein, op. cit., p. 233.
[3] Ibid., p. 16.

. . . The Romantic musician considered those of his works the most noble that were the most purposeless.'

The gap between the composer and the ordinary tune-loving listener began to widen as soon as music ceased to be written to order. 'Alas,' cried Berlioz, 'if one could only reduce the public to an assembly of fifty sensible and intelligent persons, how bliss-ful it would be to be an artist!'[1] (It is a far cry from Mozart's descriptions of the crowded audience at *The Magic Flute*. 'I have this moment returned from the opera, which was as full as ever,' he wrote to his wife in October 1791. 'As usual the duet "Mann und Weib" and Papageno's "Glockenspiel" in Act I had to be repeated, and also the trio of the boys in Act II. But what always gives me most pleasure is the silent approval. You can see how the opera is becoming more and more popular . . .')

Purposeless music put an end to the practical attitude of mind that had enabled Haydn to polish the buttons on his uniform before playing in his newest string quartet for the Esterházy house-party. 'The creator of music,' we are told by Einstein,[2] 'who as late as the eighteenth century had been little more than a craftsman, became himself . . . a Romantic figure. Goethe had given the Romantics a fictional model with his Wilhelm Meister, [and] now . . . when the heroes of novels were not specifically musicians, they were usually at least artists, mostly unfit for life.'

The romantic Romantics had no hesitation in getting rid of the old-fashioned eighteenth-century balance of thought and feel-ing. 'Only in music does feeling, actually and radiantly present . . . dispense with the help of reason.' It is Liszt who is speaking.[3] He goes on to say that while listening to instrumental music he feels 'a liberation of the soul . . . Released from all material fetters, [it] resigns itself unhampered to emotion's endless sea.' (One wonders what the orchestral players thought about it all. Did they also experience a liberation of the soul, or were they too much hampered by the material necessity of having to turn over the pages and play the right notes?)

'Emotion's endless sea' is only another name for what Sir Maurice Bowra describes as 'the German respect for unsatisfied

---

[1] Strunk, op. cit., p. 826.
[2] Einstein, op. cit., p. 345.
[3] Strunk, op. cit., p. 850.

longing as an end in itself'. It is an immense relief to find Schumann exclaiming: 'How I wish some young composer would sometime give us a gay, light symphony, in a major key!'[1]

Composers, however, preferred to use the orchestra for its 'immeasurable capacity for the expression of impulses and desires of elemental intensity', a capacity which Wagner declared had been 'opened up by Beethoven'. [2]

'To the Romantics', says Einstein,[3] 'instrumental music became the choicest means of saying what could not be said, of expressing something deeper than the *word* had been able to express. . . . They felt that Beethoven was especially "deep"— because they did not quite understand him.'

Romantic depth encouraged vagueness. Berlioz, in his description of *Roméo et Juliette*, extolled the language of instruments above all other languages, finding it 'richer, more varied, more free from limitations, and—in its very vagueness—incomparably more powerful'.[4]

But tunes cannot thrive on vagueness. They need a clear outline and a definite purpose. And a real tune, with a beginning and a middle and an end, would have been uncomfortably out of place in emotion's endless sea. When the romantic composer of symphonic tone poems wanted his listeners to recognize what was happening, he found it safer to use leitmotives as signposts. And he took the precaution of providing abundant programme notes. In Liszt's own explanation of his *Berg-Sinfonie*[5] we are told that 'the poet hears two voices, one infinite, magnificent, ineffable, singing the beauty and harmony of creation, the other swollen with sighs, with groans, with sobs, with rebellious cries, and with blasphemous oaths. The one is saying "Nature"; the other "Humanity".'

Wagner's leitmotives can be whistled, but they cannot be rounded off with the satisfaction of a real tune's homecoming. In *Die Meistersinger*, the diatonic songs and dances are straightforward and persistent, but in some of the chromatic works the

---

[1] Schumann, op. cit., p. 77.
[2] *Das Kunstwerk der Zukunft*, quoted by Strunk, op. cit., p. 891.
[3] Einstein, op. cit., pp. 32–3.
[4] Ibid., p. 140.
[5] Ibid., p. 69.

harmony becomes so diffused that it can no longer provide the foundation for a clear melodic line. The 'endless melody' of *The Ring* cannot be taken home and sung in solitude, for it is so saturated with its own harmonies that it refuses to sort itself out into a single thread that can be grasped hold of. Even the memorable opening of *Tristan* is impossible to sing. The first three notes are easy enough, for they stand out, naked and expressive. But when it comes to the fourth note, where the voice longs to fall another semitone, the 'upper outline of the chords' wanders off on rising chromatic passing-notes that are meaningless without their harmonies.

Wagner himself would have had little sympathy with those in the audience who were just waiting for the heroine's next song; we are told that when his friend Friedrich Nietzsche showed too much interest in what was happening on the stage during *Tristan*, Wagner leant across to him and whispered: 'Take off your spectacles! You must hear nothing but the orchestra!'[1]

Nineteenth-century audiences in search of a tune chose to listen to Italian opera, where the singers still had arias, as in the days of the Camerata. Or they went to the ballet, where they were given gloriously simple tunes that had to be definite and obvious to allow the dancers to count their eights securely:

Ex. 178

Trepak, from 'Casse-Noisette'   Tchaikovsky

[1] Ibid., p. 240.

This direct descendant of Kodály's Mari folk song in Chapter II is a welcome reminder that good tunes are built to last. And there must have been many listeners in the first-night St. Petersburg audience in December 1892 who felt, as they heard it, that this was their sort of music.

CHAPTER XII

Today's Tunes

Unfortunately', wrote Parry in the first edition of Grove's *Dictionary of Music*, 'the material of the simpler order of melody tends to be exhausted.'

This remark is reprinted, just as it stands, in the 1954 edition of Grove, although there have been more memorable English tunes written during the twentieth century than at any other time since the death of Purcell. But Parry, at the time when he wrote that article on 'Melody', could hardly have avoided a hint of pessimism, for in the eighteen-eighties there were few tonic-and-dominant tunes strong enough to stand on their own feet. Even the tunes of the Anglican chants in the church services were becoming so clogged with chromaticism that they could find little room for any more semitones:

Ex. 179

(Praise him in the sound of the trumpet: praise him upon the
lute and harp.
Praise him in the cymbals and dances: praise him upon the
strings and pipe, etc.)

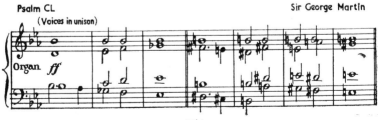

(in harmony)

The dismal scarcity of good nineteenth-century English tunes must have been as baffling to Parry as it is to twentieth-century historians. Why were there no contemporary settings of poems by Keats and Shelley, or by Wordsworth and Tennyson? Why was there no young composer among those friends of Gwen Raverat's uncle Richard, who used to 'wait outside the book shops in the early morning, when they heard that a new volume of Tennyson was to come out'?[1]

And why is it Purcell left no musical heir to carry on from where he had left off at the end of the seventeenth century?

It is true that the stream of English tunes never quite dried up; Carey, Arne, Boyce, Dibdin and Wesley each contributed to it. But after the inundation of the sixteenth and seventeenth centuries, the eighteenth-century stream is distressingly small. And by the nineteenth century it shrinks to a trickle, with 'Home, sweet Home' at one end and Gilbert and Sullivan at the other. The most memorable of the tunes that were sung and played in nineteenth-century homes were folk songs from Scotland and Ireland: they had been collected from traditional singers and arranged with simple piano accompaniments.

Nineteenth-century choral societies kept themselves in existence by singing Handel's *Messiah* year after year. There were enough good tunes in the work to satisfy them for the rest of their lives, and they saw no reason for singing anything else.

Serious students left England for Germany, where music was the native language. And when they had returned home, they brought up their children or their pupils in the firm belief that music meant German music. They also helped to spread the belief that music had progressed from a barbarous past through increasingly enlightened stages (with Haydn preparing the way for Beethoven) until it had finally reached its culmination in the

[1] Gwen Raverat, *Period Piece*, Faber & Faber, London, 1952, p. 126.

second half of the nineteenth century. It is only natural that they should have felt like that about the exciting times they were living through. What is surprising is that their belief should have persisted well into the twentieth century, so that we find as great an historian as Einstein declaring on the last page of his 1947 *Music in the Romantic Era* that 'the music of the Romantic period is *our* music'. He does not say for whom he is speaking, but it is not for those of us in England who have been brought up from the age of three on the tunes of Purcell.

At school I had lessons from a piano teacher who had been a pupil of Clara Schumann: she had had to practise Brahms's rhapsodies with Brahms sitting in the next room. It was enthralling to be given Schumann's own advice about playing the tunes in *Carnaval* and the G minor sonata. But even at the height of the excitement, I never felt like saying 'this is *our* music'. For I had already had ten years of humming Purcell's tunes at home, beginning with 'Hither this way', because my father happened to have been doing *King Arthur* that year with his students at Morley College.

He himself had only discovered Purcell after years of ardent Wagner-worship. Every moment of his life as a student had been filled with the remembered sound of Wagner's chromatic sequences. When he was asked to train the newly formed Socialist choir in William Morris's house in Hammersmith, he inevitably gave them Wagner choruses to learn, using English translations that had to be sung to be believed.

It was the translations from the German that did most damage to the songs which the young English composers of the nineties were trying to write. The tunes sounded instrumental with their foreign accentuation, and self-consciousness showed through each well-meaning attempt at nobility or pathos. Elgar's 'Land of Hope and Glory' was fated to sound as it does, with the stressed and unstressed syllables of 'glory' evenly ironed out, and with the rising phrase giving the word 'and' an unwanted prominence which is further emphasized by the falling fourth that follows it. Heard side by side with 'Fairest Isle', the tune is a convincing proof of the need for expressing the energy of English words.

Elgar and his younger contemporaries had to start more or less from the beginning. They had lost the use of their own language in music, and no one had suggested to them that they should try coupling their words and notes lovingly together, or that they might first feel the gesture of a sentence and then learn to follow it in sound.

It was many years before my father could realize what the trouble had been. 'Never having managed to learn a foreign language', he wrote to a friend in 1917, 'songs had always meant to me a peg of words on which to hang a tune. The great awakening came on hearing the recitatives in Purcell's *Dido*. Can you or anyone tell me how he managed *straight away* to write the only really musical idiom of the English language we have yet had?'

The underlining of the 'straight away' shows that he and his friends took it for granted that tunes and words could not sound at one with each other until after a long struggle. The revival of English folk songs, as well as the republication of Purcell and the English lutenist composers, helped them to recognize the musical possibilities of their own language. My father used to say that after the publication of Fellowes's edition of Morley's madrigals he had 'never been quite the same man'. Because of this wild enthusiasm he often seemed to me to exaggerate the significance of the revival of English music: I can remember feeling embarrassed during his lectures in the early nineteen twenties whenever I heard him say that the most important thing for English composers was to get to know the great English music of the past. But I can now realize that he was right to be so over-insistent at that time, and the only reason I felt embarrassed was that I took it for granted that Dowland was as great a song-writer as Schubert, and couldn't see why there was any need to have it pointed out.

To the English composers of fifty years ago, it seemed as if the revival of folk song might also help to solve the problem of how to get rid of all the old, unwanted associations of major and minor keys and their chromatic passing-notes. Obviously it was impossible to go back to writing tunes as 'normal' as Handel's, after having lived through the excitement of Wagner's chromaticism. And it was impossible to write bigger and better chromatic sequences, because Wagner had already gone as far as anyone could go in that direction.

To escape from key-notes and key-relationships seemed essential in the late nineteen twenties, in England as in other countries. One blushed, during a Queen's Hall concert of new music, if the instruments of the orchestra inadvertently drew together on to a chord of the dominant seventh.

Folk tunes, which had been born before keys were invented, seemed at first to point the way to salvation. But although their modality was helpful in the earliest stages of the English upheaval, the tunes were unable to solve every problem. They had a way of sticking out, indigestibly, in music that had been constructed on nineteenth-century symphonic lines. And their diatonic austerity could not provide a lasting substitute for the emotional warmth and colour of the bad old days. So English composers, like those elsewhere in Europe, were driven to experiment.

They explored, among other things, the possibilities of polytonality. Ex. 180 is one of the three-key canons that my father wrote, somewhat apologetically, at the end of his life. He had to make the songs reasonably simple, as they were written for amateurs in schools and colleges. The voices sing their straightforward tune in each of its orthodox keys, but the blend of the different keys gives the music the expressive colour of chromaticism without any of its nineteenth-century associations. And when the voices meet together on their triads, the sound has the welcoming freshness of rediscovery:

Ex. 180

From 'Six Canons for Equal Voices'   Gustav Holst

'Lovely Venus' was one of the many compromises that helped in the struggle. By the nineteen thirties, first-night audiences at Queen's Hall could once more listen unabashed to major and minor triads. English music had shaken off the worst of its self-consciousness and it had also managed to get rid of some of the notions that had been so near to the hearts of the romantic Romantics. Instrumental tunes were no longer considered superior to songs on account of their 'vagueness'. There was no need for music to be 'purposeless': it could, in fact, be written for school-children and church festivals and brass bands and for any other amateurs in need of a good tune to sing or play. Composers felt less ashamed about borrowing from each other's music, and the 'desperate independence' of the nineteenth century no longer mattered quite so much. So that by the time Britten wrote his song cycle to celebrate the two hundred and fiftieth anniversary of the death of Purcell, he was able to be as 'obvious' as he liked:

Ex. 181

From The Holy Sonnets of John Donne   Britten

The gesture and the energy have been learnt from Purcell,
but the language is Britten's own, and it takes what it needs
from all that has happened in music since 1695, including the
riches of Mahler and the sonority of the modern piano.

It is the directness and obviousness of his tunes that makes it possible for amateurs to perform the music he writes for them. At the earliest rehearsals for the first performance of *Noye's Fludde* the Suffolk schoolchildren were able to sing and play their overwhelmingly dramatic storm music with a virtuoso assurance. Each performer is given what he can enjoy doing, including the members of the audience, whose unrehearsed but confident entry of 'Eternal Father' at the height of the storm provides the musical climax of the drama. The hymn tune is not served out to the audience as a separate number; it is woven into the orchestral texture of the storm with the organized deliberation of an extended chorale in a Bach cantata. And, as a result, the 'dated' modulations of the nineteenth-century hymn never sound out of place.

Britten is always aware of the extraordinary adaptability of 'obvious' tunes, whatever century they may belong to. In his music, everything goes with everything else, which is why the Rustics' parodies in the last act of *A Midsummer Night's Dream* belong to the music of the whole opera, instead of standing out in isolation. Pyramus, in his aria addressed to Wall, can indulge in sequence after sequence with a modulating fervour that comes near to bursting-point, but his tune goes with all the other tunes, and its nineteenth-century chromaticism is on the friendliest of terms with the subtler chromaticism of the lullaby at the end of Act II:

Ex. 182

From Act II of A Midsummer Night's Dream Britten

The semitones in Ex. 182 have none of the vagueness of the early twentieth-century passing-notes that used to flavour the diatonic outline of a simple tune as if they were still yearning for the lost chromaticism of Wagner. 'All shall be well' is utterly undisturbed by any thought of Wagner, just as the twelve-note tunes in Britten's recent works are undisturbed by any thought of Schoenberg. The structural fourths and fifths of the twelve-note theme in *The Turn of the Screw* bear the weight of the whole opera owing to their strength as pivots in the circle of key-relationships. And in the light-hearted *Cantata Academica* the equally structural note-row emerges as a triumphant tune for an amateur chorus:

Ex. 183

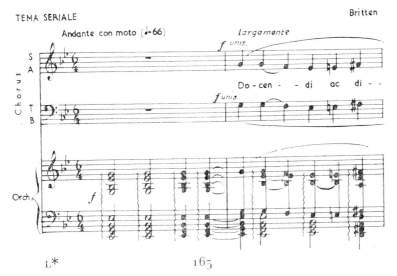

The tune keeps to the orthodox serial pattern, using each semitone within the octave and avoiding going back on any note until
all the twelve have been passed through. But it is as different
from Schoenberg as it could possibly be. For the notes, far from
being related only to each other, are passionately loyal to their
tonic. The straightforward seven-note major scale, stretched to
embrace the remaining five semitones, provides such an obviously
singable tune that many of the audience, after the first English
performance, were humming it as they pushed their way out
into the damp November night.

Schoenberg would have liked to hear his audiences hum his
tunes. 'I want people to know and whistle my melodies,' he
wrote in 1947, 'I don't want to be interesting.'[1]

He could hardly have escaped being 'interesting' when he had
discovered a way of reorganizing the construction of melodic lines
after the chaos of atonality. In his 'method of composing with
twelve notes which are related only with one another' he had, in
his own words, 'laid the foundations for a new procedure in
musical construction which seemed fitted to replace those structural differentiations provided formerly by tonal harmonies'.[2]

This twelve-note method of writing had offered an entirely new
solution to the early twentieth-century problem of getting rid of

[1] Quoted by Hans Keller in *The New Statesman*, 6 February 1960.
[2] J. Rufer, *Composition with Twelve Notes*, trans. Humphrey Searle, Rockliff,
London, 1954, p. 5.

the unwanted associations of tonality. The chromatically-minded composers of previous centuries had never thought of using the notes of the chromatic scale as raw material for making tunes. When Bach chose to use eleven of the twelve notes, one after another, without going back on any note, he was embroidering the modulations of his harmony:

Ex. 184

From the 1st.Kyrie in the B minor Mass

Here the 'pull towards the tonal centre' is as obvious as in Britten's 'Tema Seriale' (Ex. 183).

In Schoenberg's melodies 'each note has a definite interval-relationship to the notes which precede and follow it'. But the ordinary listener in the audience, who is, after all, the potential hummer of tunes, has no way of recognizing the relationship, and when the performance is over, he pushes his way out, either in silence, or else muttering, with the ghosts of Roger North's friends, the age-long complaint: 'Wee do not understand this.'

In every generation there are the same complaints about 'lack of tunefulness' or 'too much distortion'. Artusi, in 1600, was complaining that Monteverdi and his contemporaries would 'perhaps so exert themselves that in the course of time they will discover a new method by which dissonance will become consonance and consonance dissonance'.[1] It sounds far-fetched, but I have known it happen in twentieth-century music. During a rehearsal I once found myself accusing a distinguished tenor of singing an out-of-tune octave in the middle of a long unaccompanied passage consisting almost entirely of minor ninths, major sevenths and tritones: he was singing it perfectly in tune, but the ear had grown so accustomed to the inevitable dissonances that when the unexpected consonance occurred it sounded wrong.

This particular problem of intonation could never arise in twelve-note music, where the octave is avoided on account of its obviousness. Perfect fifths are also avoided, as they too are

[1] Strunk, op. cit., p. 400.

'obvious in the acoustic sense of the overtones near to the funda-
mental'.[1] This avoidance of the familiar 'landing-stages' of a tune
makes it difficult for untrained audiences to seize hold of any
twelve-note theme at a first hearing.

The listener who tries to follow the sound of the less obvious
twelve-note intervals is faced with the added difficulty of the
wide gaps between the notes:

Ex. 185

From the Wind Quintet, Op. 26   Schoenberg

It would make the melody much easier to whistle if one could
begin by practising it with the widest intervals reduced to a more
manageable level, and with enharmonic changes to simplify the
written appearance:

Ex. 185a

But this utterly destroys Schoenberg's intentions. The relaxed
intervals slip back into an unavoidably tonal frame of mind in
which every falling semitone hints at a suspension, and unless one
is careful the tune gets out of control and turns itself into the sort
of waltz that one of Chopin's admirers might have written a
hundred years ago:

Ex. 186

con ped.

---

[1] H. H. Stuckenschmidt, *Arnold Schoenberg*, John Calder, London, 1959,
p. 135.

166

Since wide intervals are essential in twelve-note music, we must be prepared for long stretches of unrelieved tension. The tension is not always apparent when the learner is trying out the notes on the piano, for there is no physical difference in approaching high notes or low notes on a keyboard. But a horn player knows all about the physical difference in tension between a minor second and a minor ninth. And a sympathetic listener, with muscles as taut as a dancer's, may be willing to respond with his whole being to the waves of sound that break over him, but if he is offered nothing but widely-spaced dissonances his nerves will be unequal to the strain, and he will have to let the intervals slide off him for the sake of self-preservation.

To be unconcerned about tension and relaxation in music is to forget the meaning of its language. And that is perhaps why the ordinary listener finds it difficult to hum Schoenberg's music: he misses the essential ingredient in the rise and fall of 'Co-erl' in Ex. 6.

Another reason that twelve-note melodies are difficult to learn is their refusal to go back on a note. There is no twelve-note equivalent of 'Sally go round the moon' (Ex. 17) for twentieth-century five-year-olds to begin on.

To go back on a note is to emphasize it, and Schoenberg has stated that 'an emphasized note could be interpreted as a root or even a tonic: the consequences . . . must be avoided'.[1]

By banishing the tonic in its function of a key-note, the twelv note composers have also got rid of it in its function of a dron which existed long before keys were thought of. It is the long-held Sa of the Indian tampura that makes it possible for the European listener to follow the Hindola raga in Exs. 73 and 74, where the intervals of the five-note basic row have little in common with our major or minor scale. And it is the 'earlier-than-key' tonic that provides the starting-note for the pentatonic tunes in Chapter II, where the widest gapped intervals can be found with

[1] Rufer, op. cit., p. 90.

ease because the notes are already lying waiting within the familiar pattern of the mode.

The wide gaps in twelve-note music are also lying waiting to be sung or played, for composers and performers have to make themselves as familiar with the shape of their basic note-row as the Mari folk singers were familiar with the shape of their pentatonic scale. If a twelve-note work has vitality as well as skill, its performers can feel the tension and relaxation of each interval according to its meaning in the context, and they can experience each subtle relationship of rhythm and form.

But the 'less learned' in the audience cannot hope to grasp the note-row as if it were a mode, for the series of notes changes with each work, and it is never displayed beforehand with the slow, deliberate unfolding that introduces each raga.

'Essentially listeners to music become more specialized and thus more limited,' writes Stuckenschmidt in his book on Schoenberg.[1] The words are not Schoenberg's own, but he would probably have agreed with them, for, in spite of wanting to have his melodies whistled, we are told that he never felt very strongly about the contact between composer and audience, or, indeed, between composer and performer. Stuckenschmidt mentions a discussion that he had with him in 1949:

'When the conversation turned on *Moses und Aaron*, and the author suggested that the work should be quickly completed, so that it could be performed in Germany, Schoenberg energetically parried the idea. It was not being written with the idea of performances; he even felt that in part it could not be performed at all. Perhaps some time, in the distant future, with synthetic electronic means.

'This belief in a Utopian technical progress, coupled with a supreme indifference about having his works performed, is typical of Schoenberg. Both show the same attitude for which Beethoven found the famous words: "What do I care about this wretched fiddle when the spirit comes over me?"[2] Brahms, when advised to listen to a performance of *Don*

---

[1] Stuckenschmidt, op. cit., p. 136.

[2] 'Wass glaubt er, dass ich an seine elende Geige denke, wenn der Geist mich packt?' Quoted by Schoenberg in his *Style and Idea*, Williams and Norgate, London, 1951.

Giovanni at the Vienna Opera, declared that he heard the best performance when he read the score.'[1]

This is the widening of the gap between the professional artist and the amateur that Schumann warned his students about, when he assured them that there had never been a time when art had really flourished without a give-and-take between the two. And this, surely, is the chief reason that Schoenberg's tunes are not whistled in the street.

Meanwhile, the ordinary listener still asks for music with a tune in it. And just at present he is getting more tunes from England than from anywhere else.

'Why is this country still relatively unserial?' asks Hans Keller.[2] He goes on to say: 'I would suggest that a composer can afford to be as unserial as he is naturally monothematic. There is no strong sonata tradition in this country; in the circumstances, thematicism will go a long way.'

There is certainly no strong sonata tradition in England: there is hardly any sonata tradition at all, just as there is practically no romantic tradition. Our two hundred years of comparative silence may have been disheartening while they lasted, but they have meant that we have had far less than the Germans and Austrians to recover from and to rebel against. The chromatic incongruity of the chant in Ex. 179 can be swept aside and forgotten in thirty seconds, but the chromaticism of *Tristan* was sufficiently potent to have caused a large-scale revolution.

In England we still have a good deal to live through before we need to begin worrying about throwing everything overboard. And it is difficult to agree with Parry that the raw material for simple tunes is becoming exhausted. Even the scale of C shows little sign of wearing out.

It is encouraging to be told that if the four descending notes at the beginning of the change-ringing in Ex. 1 were to be increased to an octave and a half, it would take the twelve ringers thirty-eight years to get through their 479,001,600 patterns before they got back to the beginning again.

It looks as though Roger North's 'fund of all pleasing tune' can be dipped into for some time to come.

[1] Stuckenschmidt, op. cit., p. 147.
[2] From an article in the Aldeburgh Festival Programme Book, 1960.

Acknowledgments to Sources

———— ❧ ————

I wish to express my thanks to the following, who have kindly allowed me to reproduce copyright material: to Miss Emily Anderson, for permission to quote from her translation of *The Letters of Mozart and his Family* (Macmillan, 1938); to Arno Volk-Verlag, Köln, for two music examples from *Europäischer Volksgesang*, ed. Wiora; to Edward Arnold Ltd., for leave to quote from E. M. Forster's *Aspects of the Novel*; to Dr. Marius Barbeau of the Canadian Folk Music Society, for the 'Fireweed Song', published in the *Musical Quarterly* for January 1931; to Barrie Books Ltd. for extracts from Zoltán Kodály's *Folk Music of Hungary* and J. Rufer's *Composition with Twelve Notes* (both of these in conjunction with the Macmillan Company of New York), and from Ferruccio Busoni's *The Essence of Music* (with the Philosophical Library, New York); to G. Bell and Sons for quotations from *Schumann's Early Letters*, translated by May Herbert, which appeared in Bohn's Library; to Boosey and Hawkes for allowing me to give examples from the works of Benjamin Britten; to Messrs. Breitkopf and Härtel and British and Continental Music Agencies Ltd. for an extract from Spitta's edition of Schütz's works, and for an example from *Altdeutsches Liederbuch*, ed. Böhme; to the Buchan Club, Peterhead, for the tune 'Lord Brechin'; to Mr. John Bunting of Barrie Books for examples from Alain Daniélou's *Northern Indian Music*; to John Calder Ltd. for two quotations from *Arnold Schoenberg*, by H. H. Stuckenschmidt; to J. Curwen and Sons Ltd., for extracts from Christopher Simpson's *The Division Viol* and for my father's 'Lovely Venus'; to the Librairie Delagrave, Paris, for permission to quote from an article by Knosp in the *Encyclopédie de la Musique*; to J. M. Dent and Sons Ltd. for a number of extracts from Curt Sachs, *The Rise of Music in the Ancient World*, from *The Bach Reader*, from Alfred Einstein's *Music in the Romantic Era* (all these three in conjunction with W. W. Norton and Co. Inc. of New York), and from Otto Deutsch's *Schubert, A Documentary Biography*; to Dennis Dobson for four extracts from Schumann's *On Music and Musicians*, translated by P. Rosenfeld, and for two from Eric Werner's *The Sacred Bridge*; to the English Folk Dance and Song Society for allowing me to reproduce tunes from their Journals; to the Harvard University Press for extracts from Igor Stravinsky's *Poetics of Music*; to Hinrichsen Edition Ltd. for leave to include part of Hugo Wolf's 'Das verlassene Mägdlein' from *Mörike-Lieder*; to Holt, Rinehart and Winston, Inc., New York, for quotations from Idelsohn's *Jewish Music*; to the Hutchinson Publishing Group for a quotation from Denis Stevens's *A History of Song*; to Burns and Oates Ltd. and the Indiana University Press for music examples and extracts from the text of Apel's *Gregorian Chant*; to Universal Edition (Alfred A. Kalmus Ltd.) for extracts from the Malipiero Edition of the works of Monteverdi and from Schoenberg's Wind Quintet (Op. 26); to Miss Maud Karpeles for the tunes of 'The Seeds of Love'; to Mrs. C. J. A. Kunst-van Wely for permission to quote from her late husband's *A Study on Papuan Music*; to Macmillan and Co. Ltd. for extracts from *Grove's Dictionary of Music and Musicians*; to the Mercury Music Corporation, New York, for an example from Josquin's 'Salve Regina', ed. David; to the Merlin Press for a reference to G. B. Chambers's *Folksong—Plainsong*; to Mrs. Mertis Morehead of Shreveport, Louisiana, for an extract from *Traditional Ballads mainly from West Virginia*, collected by her brother, the late John Harington Cox; to the Editor of the *New Statesman* for permission to quote from an article by Hans Keller, 6 February 1960; to Novello and Co. Ltd. for the tunes 'Sally go round the Moon', 'Shallow Brown', 'Nottamun Town' and 'I gave my Love a Cherry', for quotations from the text of *Roger North on Music*, for an extract from my father's *Choral Symphony*, and for a chant from *The New Cathedral Psalter*; to the Oxford University Press, London, for permission to include music examples from *The New Oxford History of Music*, from *Studies in African Music* by A. M. Jones, from the *Harvard Anthology*, from *Tudor Church Music*, ed.

Fellowes, and from my own *Singing for Pleasure*; and extracts from the text of two of the above, as well as from C. M. Bowra, *The Romantic Imagination*, from C. S. Terry, *Bach's Orchestra*, from *Henry Purcell, Essays on his Music* and from my *Gustav Holst, A Biography*; also to the Clarendon Press, Oxford, for short quotations from Wellesz, *A History of Byzantine Music and Hymnography*, and from *The Apocryphal New Testament*, translated by M. R. James; to Penguin Books Ltd. for a quotation from *The Pelican History of Music*; to the Royal Music Association for Dunstable's 'Ave maris stella' from *Musica Britannica*; to Stainer and Bell Ltd. for the music examples in Chapter 6; to Verlagsanstalt Tyrolia, Innsbruck, for a tune from *Echte Tiroler Lieder*; to the Vereniging voor Nederlandse Muziekgeschiedenis, The Hague, for leave to quote from an article by the late Jaap Kunst in their Kongressbericht, 1952; and to the Yale University Press for permission to include part of the Léonin 'Alleluia' from Waite's *The Rhythm of Twelfth-Century Polyphony*.

I must also thank Faber and Faber Ltd. for allowing me to include examples from Oliver Strunk's *Source Readings in Music History*, and quotations from the text of Gwen Raverat's *Period Piece* and Shattuck's *The Banquet Years*.

I am particularly grateful to Jonathan Steele for his help in the transcription of plainsong into modern notation, to Rosamund Strode for copying manuscripts from the British Museum, and to my secretary, Elizabeth Edwards, for her criticisms and her help in translating from Latin, Italian and French.

Index

(Music examples are indicated by page numbers in italic type.)

Index